GARDENS
of Northumberland
and the Borders

by Susie White   Photographs by Simon Fraser

"WHEN WEARIED AND OVER-WROVGHT BY
STVDY OR AFFAIRS OF BVSINESS REPAIR
TO THESE HAVNTS AND REFRESH YOVR
MIND BY A STROLL AMIDST THE FLOWERS

First published in Great Britain in 2006 by Sanderson Books Limited.
Text and photographs copyright Susie White, Simon Fraser and Sanderson Books Limited, 2006.

Text by Susie White / www.chesterswalledgarden.co.uk
Photography by Simon Fraser / www.simonfraserphoto.com
Designed by Sokell Design / www.sokell.com
Editor: Catherine Sanderson
Colour reproduction by Dot Gradations Ltd, UK
Printed and Bound in Italy.
Set in Goudy Old Style

Other titles published by Sanderson Books Limited:
Northumberland ISBN 0954802403
Newcastle upon Tyne ISBN 09548024-1-1
Holy Island of Lindisfarne ISBN 095480242X
Bamburgh, Seahouses and The Farne Islands ISBN 0954802438

Sanderson Books Limited
Front Street, Klondyke, Cramlington, Northumberland, NE23 6RF

ISBN 0954802446

Half-title page: Halls of Heddon - Dahlias are good for attracting butterflies - this one is the collerette 'Pooh'.

Facing title page: Wallington - Red squirrels can be easily spotted from the woodland bird hide.

Title page: Wallington - An invitation to 'stroll amidst the flowers'.

Below: Abbotsford - The Morris Garden.

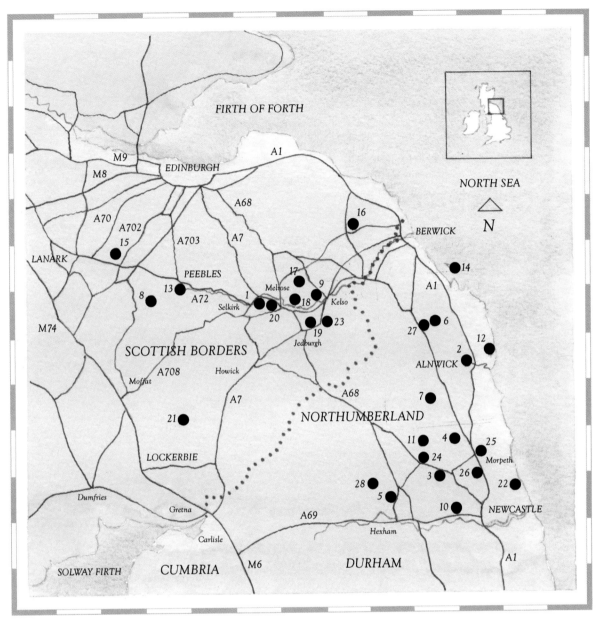

Map © Mike Weaver

Garden Locations

1 Abbotsford
2 The Alnwick Garden
3 Belsay Hall
4 Bide-A-Wee Cottage
5 Chesters Walled Garden
6 Chillingham Castle
7 Cragside
8 Dawyck Botanic Garden
9 Floors Castle
10 Halls of Heddon

11 Herterton House
12 Howick Hall
13 Kailzie
14 Lindisfarne Castle Garden
15 Little Sparta
16 Manderston
17 Mellerstain
18 Mertoun
19 Monteviot
20 Priorwood and Harmony

21 Samye Ling
22 Seaton Delaval Hall
23 Teviot Water Gardens
24 Wallington
25 William Turner Garden
26 Blagdon Hall
27 Lilburn Tower
28 Nunwick

Contents

Foreword by Lord Howick

W̱E DON'T ALWAYS THINK of Northumberland and the Scottish Borders as ideal country for gardeners, but Susie White has written a book that not only disproves this but also gives us good reason to be proud of our achievements. From the large and the new to the small and the old, there is as wide a variety of styles and traditions as any garden visitor could want, while owners vary from the institutional, like the National Trust at Wallington and Cragside or the Royal Botanic Gardens Edinburgh at Dawyck, to the intimate creations of individuals at Bide-A-Wee, and Chesters Walled Garden created by Susie White.

Of course we do have the advantage over much of the south of more open space with fewer people, and most of these gardens are sited in countryside often worth visiting for its own merits. There are many interesting examples of how gardeners have tackled the twin problems of soil and climate, often with ingenuity and always with great effect. I was brought up on the cardinal rule of planting out of the Northumberland wind and that is a common feature throughout the area in this book. Frank Lawley at Herterton House, however, proves how much can be achieved on exposed sites.

I have great pleasure in commending this book to the reader and I hope that he or she will derive as much benefit as I have from visiting the many gardens of great quality so admirably described by the author.

opposite: *Autumn at Howick Hall*

Introduction

WITH RICHLY VARYING LANDSCAPES, the two adjacent counties of Northumberland and the Scottish Borders have a unique quality and a wonderful array of fascinating gardens. From the windswept, rugged outlook of Lindisfarne to the sheltered quarry garden at Belsay, from the cold glen and wooded slopes of Dawyck to the Victorian walled garden of Cragside, it is the land itself that has influenced their development. Finding ways of creating shelter for growing has resulted in beautiful woodlands and magnificent walled gardens. The underlying stone has been used to build romantic castles or carefully quarried out to make microclimates in which gardens could flourish. There are new gardens too, with Alnwick and Little Sparta drawing worldwide attention to this diverse region. The best of them have been drawn together for this book.

Peace only came to the Borders region in the seventeenth century, and before that the Debatable Lands, as they were known, were constantly contested and fought over. Even modest houses had to be defensive; castles abound, from the grandest such as Alnwick to the smallest Pele towers. Only as life became more peaceable, could gardens eventually be created, which is why the earliest existing features are usually from the eighteenth century. If there were any earlier versions, they were usually swept away by 'Capability' Brown or his school. What this gives us, in garden terms, is often fabulous backdrops to the planting: the sheer castle walls of Chillingham, the huge and impressive mansions of Manderston and Mellerstain.

I came to live in Northumberland nearly thirty years ago and immediately fell for the wide skies and for the wild moorland threaded with secluded valleys. There is an ever-present sense of history, from the switchback curves of Hadrian's Wall to the defensive houses known as Bastles. With my daughter born in Edinburgh, I also have a strong affinity with the Scottish Borders and the beguiling landscapes of the Tweed and Teviot. Having gardened here for all that time, twenty years of it spent creating Chesters Walled Garden, I have had many happy times in other people's gardens throughout every season; glimpsing deer in the snowbound woods of Wallington, walking down to the sea from Howick Hall with my children in summer.

It has been such a pleasure to write this book; to re-visit places that have meant a lot to me and to discover a few gardens that I had not been to before but had always heard about. Most of them are open regularly, but there are three exceptions that are so special, I felt I must include them. These are only open occasionally for charity, so please check when they are open.

Gardeners are so welcoming and happy to talk about how they do it all; there is much to learn from them. If there is one thing that unifies the gardens in this region, it is the need to protect our plants from the weather. Choosing the right site, planting shelterbelts, building walls, and making hedges are all ways that have been used to create the right environment. Some have very difficult growing conditions; Dawyck and the garden at Samye Ling are really up against the weather. Yet somehow, the spirit to garden makes things happen and what is created is beautiful and distinct; a place to truly refresh the mind 'by a stroll amidst the flowers'.

Susie White

opposite: The curious pink spires of pokeweed,
Phytolacca clavigera, give way to first green,
then almost black berries.

Abbotsford

ABBOTSFORD IS THE ROMANTIC HOUSE built and lived in by Sir Walter Scott, author of *Rob Roy*, *Ivanhoe*, and *The Lady of the Lake*. He named it after the river crossing that was used by the monks travelling to nearby Melrose. Scott himself largely designed this miscellany of a building, completed by 1821, that includes salvaged fragments or copies of architecture: a doorway from Edinburgh's old Tolbooth, a roof from Roslin Chapel and a gateway from Linlithgow.

Since the death of Dame Jean Maxwell-Scott in 2004, Scott's last direct descendant, the house and garden have been managed by executors and with increased but sensitive publicity, the garden is being revitalised. It was Sir Walter Scott who first laid out the garden, into three separate areas, the South Court by the house, the Morris Garden, and the walled garden with its pretty orangery. The visitor entrance to the house is down steep steps under a short tunnel and then along a sunken, moat-like walk. A line of cloister arches, through which red roses peep, frames one side of the South Court.

A calm, monastic space with lawns and topiary yew trees, the south court has a central basin on a stepped plinth. This once stood in the Tolbooth in Edinburgh and in 1660 was filled with wine for the people to drink from on the Restoration of Charles II. Red fuchsias and carnations are planted around it to mimic the wine, with silver curry plant and euonymus at its base. On two sides, a tall yew hedge grows hard against the stone boundary wall and has peepholes cut into it to show ancient stones collected by Scott. There are five medallions from the old Edinburgh market cross dismantled in 1756 and given to Scott by the painter, Sir Henry Raeburn. Other stones are Roman and the sculpted yew hedge becomes a charming feature.

A little bridge leads over the 'moat' and down into the Morris Garden, which is named after a character from the book, *Rob Roy*. The kneeling statue of an excise man, pleading for mercy from Helen MacGregor, is in the middle

above: *A grass path leads up to the pretty Gothic orangery.*
opposite: *The orangery is glimpsed through a round arched door in the old stone wall.*

of the lawn, and a bed of pink hardy geraniums surrounds this lichened sculpture. At one end, a little flagged path leads around the back of herbaceous borders planted with white campanulas, peonies, lilies, golden meadowsweet, and pale yellow meconopsis. It is sheltered enough to grow *Abutilon vitifolium* against the west facing wall.

From the sunken Morris Garden, the path leads into another walled garden below a round arch in the stone wall; above this is a sculpture of a bison, one of the many unusual and quirky pieces collected by Sir Walter Scott. Unusually, the walled garden is set on quite a steep slope, angled to the south and west; this gives lovely views up a double herbaceous border to the little Gothic orangery at the top. A grass path leads up the middle, the borders on either side partly symmetrical with white valerian, lemon phlomis, pink salvias, blue geraniums, and spiky sea hollies. At the front, silver and blue bedding carries on the muted colour scheme, picking up the blue and silver of white Peruvian lilies, goat's rue, and clary sage.

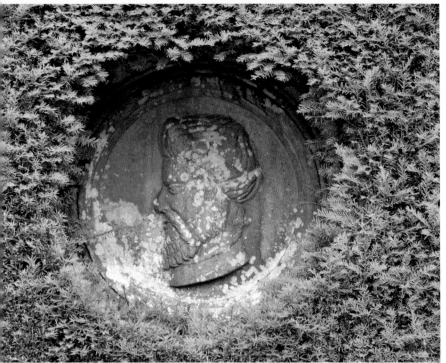

Behind the borders, the space is divided into quadrants with lawns and vegetable beds, which may be further developed into flower borders as the walled garden is redesigned. The top wall once had an integral heating system to warm it for growing fruit. There are a few old apple trees left but the west wall has been planted with new fan trained fruit trees. To either side of the orangery, there are country house borders with buddleias, bronze fennel, golden sage, globe thistles, and evening primrose. It is warm enough for pale pink cistus and (Bowles' mauve) wallflowers to grow happily here.

left (top): *Cloister arches give views into the South Court with its clipped topiary.*
left (centre): *A medallion from the old market cross in Edinburgh set into the yew hedge.*
left (bottom): *Topiary yews encircle a basin from Edinburgh's Tolbooth.*
opposite (right): *The old rose 'Dublin Bay' scrambling through decorative stonework in the South Court.*

Outside the lovely orangery are box hedges enclosing beds of Iceberg roses, which are used to make buttonholes in a continuing tradition that the lady of the house presents these to the principals of the common ridings, a beating of the bounds on horseback that is an important annual event in the Borders. Looking back down the garden from here is the best view of the house with its multi-towers and turrets, its crow-stepped gables and romantic architecture.

left: *Double herbaceous borders lead the eye down to the many-turreted house.*
below: *The exciseman's statue forms the centre piece of the Morris Garden.*

The Alnwick Garden

THE ALNWICK GARDEN IS A PHENOMENON, a remarkable twenty-first century creation on a grand scale of the kind not seen in Britain for a hundred years. It has focused attention on the gardens of Northumberland and drawn many people with its combination of innovation, fun, education, and dramatic modern design. With millions of visitors since it opened in 2001, its success has outstripped all expectations and introduced many to gardening for the first time. With new elements being added all the time, visitors are in the unique position of being able to watch its unfolding, something that would not have happened during the creation of the great gardens of the past.

The parkland surrounding Alnwick Castle was laid out in 1750 to a design by 'Capability' Brown. The flower-and-vegetable-filled walled gardens of the nineteenth century had been entirely swept away when the present Duke and Duchess of Northumberland moved to Alnwick. Seeing the state of the derelict gardens, the Duchess was inspired to create something entirely new, without simply mimicking the past. She chose world-famous Belgian landscape designer Jacques Wirtz and his son Peter to imagine something extraordinary and original.

Using the shape of the land, the Wirtz design has water as its principal theme. The walled Ornamental Garden occupies flat ground at the top of a steep slope and it is from below its network of formal rills and basins that the Grand Cascade emerges. The Cascade grows in size as it tumbles down the hillside, erupting into the foaming shapes of swirling beds, labyrinths, paths, and fountains.

The first thing the visitor sees, after emerging from the entrance pavilion, is the drama of the Cascade, which is flanked on either side by large earth banks that were constructed in the 1850s. Topped by mature trees, they create sheltering arms that embrace the curving water feature. A massive piece of construction, built from Northumberland stone, the Cascade is stepped down in a series of twenty-one weirs that sparkle and glint in the sunlight. Every minute over seven thousand gallons tumble down it, are filtered, recycled, and pumped back up again. Jets of water shoot up into the air in a complex sequence that plays every half-hour, delighting visitors, especially children, with its exuberant display.

Tunnels of hornbeam hedges weave up either side of the Cascade with 'windows' giving glimpses of the water. The sound of the waterfalls diminishes on walking uphill and entering the quieter space of the walled garden. Here it becomes a series of

right: *The breathtaking Grand Cascade at the heart of the garden.*

smooth flowing rills running happily over colourful pebbles, taking life to every part of the walled Ornamental Garden in the manner of Islamic or Paradise Gardens. Designed geometrically as a series of squares sub-divided into triangles and further squares, it is also reminiscent of medieval planting patterns. The formality is further enhanced by low box hedges and pleached fruit trees.

Wide beds around the walls are filled with colourful perennials, shrubs, and old-fashioned roses, with climbers scrambling up the brick behind. Maroon-painted dovecots are fixed high on the wall and tumbler doves swoop and preen on their little ledges. At the heart of the garden is a raised square pool, the beds around it being block planted with delphiniums, their sumptuous blue spires a reminder that water is the unifying theme. The 'rooms' and triangles created by the pleached trees and box hedges are often planted with single colours; a rich bed of silky brown irises, a triangle of purple blue salvias, a 'room' furnished in opulent deep red peonies.

At the lower end of the Cascade is a series of smaller gardens, each with a very different atmosphere. The Rose Garden is lined with pergolas so that roses assail the senses at every height. Their combined scents are exotic; their colours soft or vibrant, blooms single or blowsily full and double. All were donated by the famous rose breeder David Austin and include a rose that he named in honour of the garden, the rich pink, deeply cupped Alnwick Rose.

After the perfume and colour of the Rose Garden, the Labyrinth is a very different experience; cool and green, it is composed entirely of bamboos and ferns. These are planted on waist high banks so that the bamboos wave and arch right above head height, creating verdant tunnels, rustling in the wind.

The swirling paths are laid with brick, its pattern creating a stream-like flow. Bronze leaves set into the paths look as if they have fallen randomly from the bamboos above and the pathways lead eventually into the hub of the maze with a Latin inscription set into a stone on the floor.

left (top): *Delphiniums and roses edge a playful rill.*
left (centre): *Sinuous hedges in the Serpent Garden lead between William Pye's water sculptures.*
left (bottom): *The Alnwick rose bred by David Austin and named in honour of the garden.*
opposite: A fountain seen through the framework for the hornbeam hedge.

These curving paths are echoed in the Serpent Garden, another green space, this time made of yew and holly. Here there is a series of water sculptures created by William Pye, which explore the properties of water; it clings slickly to the underside of a polished bowl or flows smoothly over a silver ball, it rises and falls within a circular dish or mysteriously glides down two steel columns. You can even walk on water as it bubbles up under toughened glass.

Children delight in exploring amongst the twisting paths, and another interesting learning experience is in store for them in the Poison Garden. Many an adult too will be surprised by just how many common garden plants are toxic. A sinister pair of decorative black iron gates guards the entrance and proclaims 'These plants can kill'. Volunteer guides, full of information and witty anecdotes, explain to visitors the lethal qualities and histories of the poisonous plants. There is an array of famous names: henbane, deadly nightshade, hemlock, mandrake and the most poisonous British wildflower, monkshood. But there are also plants that many do not realise are dangerous; laurel which makes many a garden hedge, euphorbia, whose juice can cause temporary blindness, and comfrey, whose frequent ingestion can cause liver damage.

The dangers of drugs are highlighted, with cannabis grown here under government licence, opium poppy, which is used to make heroin and that commonly used killer, tobacco. Some of the most dangerous plants are grown under bell-shaped metal cages. The stately but toxic giant hogweed presses against the bars of its cage, trying to burst out. A snaking tunnel of ivy-covered hoops leads the visitors back out again, having been given a thought-provoking talk on the dangers of these plants.

The Alnwick Garden is about education as well as fun, and further gardens are due in the future and can be seen in the Wirtz dynamic plan. It is gardening on a massive scale unlike anything created in recent times, made all the more remarkable because we can witness its evolution.

below: *One of the many interconnecting rills and pools in the Ornamental Garden.*
opposite (top): *Cleverly pleached fruit trees against an azure spring sky.*
opposite (bottom left): *The dramatic warning on the entrance gates to the Poison Garden.*
opposite (bottom right): *The sinister deadly nightshade, Atropa belladonna.*

top: *Water cascades from the central raised pool to bubble over pebble lined rills.*

centre: *A charming spring plant, the Virginian Cowslip,* Mertensia virginica, *likes cool woodland conditions.*

bottom: *Glorious spires of delphiniums stand tall at the entrance to the Ornamental Garden.*

opposite: *White valerian flourishes below a painted dovecot.*

Belsay Hall

THE SPECTACULAR GARDENS OF BELSAY HALL were the creation of two men, Sir Charles Monck and his grandson, Sir Arthur Middleton. Although the Belsay lands have been in the Middleton family for seven centuries, these two visionary men made the house and gardens into something truly exceptional. Until the beginning of the nineteenth century, the family lived in the nearby castle, a strong, fortified Pele tower made necessary by the turbulence of the Borders region. Now partly ruined, the beautiful and dramatic castle once had formal gardens as well as a walled kitchen garden. It might have remained the family home but for Sir Charles Monck who became inspired by the architecture of ancient Greece after an extended honeymoon took him to the Mediterranean.

What he saw in Athens became an obsession, so moved was he by the controlled beauty and perfection of the buildings he saw there. He bought many books on Greek architecture and was so inspired he drew up designs for a grand country house based on the ancient classical temples of Greece. The old village of Belsay lay to the south-west of the castle, but Sir Charles had this demolished and a new village built further away. Work began on the house in 1807 and the family were able to move in to the new Hall on Christmas Day 1817. Built of warm coloured sandstone, the Hall is constructed on lines of mathematical precision and in an austere style. The Greek motifs that Sir Charles admired in Athens are present right down to the last detail.

The sandstone that the house is built from was quarried from the very rock that it stands on, from an area between the old castle and the new Hall. Even as stone was being extracted for the house, Sir Charles was thinking ahead to the shape that this would leave in the land with a view to creating a romantic garden in the ravines and rock faces of the quarry. When he went on a second Mediterranean tour in the 1830s, he was further inspired by the spectacular quarries at Siracusa with their towering pinnacles of rock. These epitomised the drama of the fashionable picturesque style, with its appearance of untamed, sublime nature. On his return to Belsay, Sir Charles constructed a massive stone arch within the quarry and planted dark-foliaged yew trees around its rim to increase the sense of depth.

Around the dramatic canyon created by the quarry, Sir Charles created woods of native trees, such as Scots pine, beech and ash. A keen horticulturalist, he planted some of the earliest introductions of monkey-puzzle trees and Douglas firs, as well as the Chusan palm, *Trachycarpus fortunei*. It is only thanks to the unusual shelter, good drainage, and dry conditions of the quarry that this can be grown so far north. For the growing of vegetables and exotic fruits for the house, Sir Charles created a walled kitchen garden with a double heated wall to make this possible. The 'hot' walls as they were known can still be seen beyond the car park at Belsay though this is all that survives. There were once buildings for growing mushrooms and storing apples, all to make the estate as self-sufficient as possible.

below: *Belsay Croquet Club on a late spring afternoon.*
opposite: *The fresh green foliage of the shuttlecock fern,* Matteuccia struthiopteris.

It was Sir Charles's grandson, Sir Arthur Middleton, who inherited the estate in 1867, his son having died. Sir Arthur was a great plantsman and, working within the layout established by his grandfather, he collected and planted a huge new range of exciting species. This was a time when many new plants were flooding in from expeditions abroad and Sir Arthur was passionate about developing the garden further. The extraction of sandstone still took place beyond the original quarry garden creating, under Sir Arthur's guidance, another canyon carefully crafted to vary in width in keeping with the original. He allowed this to be colonised by native plants, ivy, ferns, trees, and wildflowers to look as natural as possible.

Visiting Belsay today, the certain highlight is the famous quarry garden, which links the Hall with the old castle, but there is much to see on the way. A flat lawn stretches around the house emphasising its austerity, with steps descending to a lower terrace with a formal layout. Stone-edged beds are filled with the soft colours of pink roses, lady's mantle, lavender and creamy-flowered yuccas. Rich pools of purple sage billow onto the pale gravel, backed by silver Artemisias, purple cotinus and the delicate froth of *Crambe cordifolia*. The centres of the beds are raised, creating extra height, and clematis scrambles up into tall shrubs. The view from here is across a deep ha-ha to fields where sheep graze. Beyond that are the waves and mounds of a rhododendron wood, the rounded shapes punctuated by spires of conifers.

Towards the west end of the lower terrace, Sir Arthur made a snug, little garden enclosed by tall, dark yew hedges. A pair of benches is flanked by the thick, fleshy leaves of large hostas, making this a quiet, secluded place to sit especially on a hot day. Coming out into the sunshine, you emerge onto the long Magnolia Terrace.

top: *Ferns luxuriate in spring beneath blossoming rhododendrons.*
centre: *Brilliant yellow* Euphorbia polychroma *on the terrace.*
bottom: *Tall, dark conifers contrast with vibrant mounds of rhododendrons.*
opposite: *A Chusan palm can be seen through the enormous arch.*

Sheltered from the north by tall pines, a long border is a diverse mix of shrubs, roses, perennials with bulbs and dahlias. Much of the original planting, including the magnolias, had been lost, but has been restored by English Heritage working from 1940s photographs in *Country Life*. Cardoons bristle with bumblebees, buddleias, verbenas attract butterflies, and there is a smell in the air from the curious, foxy plant, *Phuopsis stylosa*.

Steps from here lead to the Winter Garden, which was created by Sir Arthur in the 1880s. This forms a large square with a sunken croquet lawn in the middle in true Victorian style. Protected from the west by a high stone wall and from north and east by pines, this must have been an unusually sheltered place for nineteenth-century ladies to promenade. In summer, you can still hear the thwack of mallet on wood as figures in white play croquet against the mown stripes of the lawn. The Winter Garden borders contain conifers, heaths and pampas grass, with some of the winter flowering heathers having been planted in 1900. Dwarf pines echo the taller trees in the wood above. The huge

west wall is draped in summer with Virginia creeper and *Vitis coignetiae*, both colouring up richly in autumn.

A small door in this wall leads towards the Quarry Garden. There is a sudden change in atmosphere away from the ordered world of the classical garden and into the wilder wood. Large ferns line the path, naturalised bulbs grow under vast beeches and the tiny pink stars of *Claytonia sibirica* sprinkle the grass. Here, there is a first glimpse of the quarried rock face, with roots of yew trees snaking down the layers of sandstone. At the base is a wildflower meadow, pretty in summer with native plants, full of snowdrops in late winter. A spreading handkerchief tree is one of Sir Arthur's important introductions. From here, the path goes deeper into the Quarry as the sides rise steeply all around. Noises are amplified and the birdsong makes it sound like being in an aviary. There is a feeling of jungle, as climbers drape their vines like lianas and ivy cascades down the rocks above the lush foliage of pokeroot.

opposite: *Emerging gunnera leaves add a touch of the tropical.*
below: *The pretty pink stars of* Claytonia sibirica, *a woodland carpeter.*

The planting is luxuriant, a mixture of exotic ferns, spreading perennials, huge gunnera leaves and shrubs such as tree peony, rhododendrons and the beautiful white flowered eucryphia. Foxgloves and other native species settle in the niches or ledges of the surrounding 'walls'. Around a bend, there are the sudden rising columns that are the entrance to the Grotto. Looking between these megaliths, there is a hint of a ferny interior; this damp-smelling enclosed space is marbled with the colours of lichens. Opposite, a little detour leads to a quiet pool flecked with green weed and overhung by large royal ferns.

The Quarry now narrows and is spanned by the massive stone arch that Sir Charles created after his visit to Siracusa. This is where the Chusan palm is able to grow, a reminder of the Mediterranean, as is a fig tree. The Quarry opens out once more with huge rock stanchions covered in the large leaved creeper, *Vitis coignetiae*. Bamboos flourish here and there is even a passion flower, remarkable so far north. The most dramatic plant in summer is the giant lily *Cardiocrinum giganteum*, growing to nearly two metres tall, sporting huge white trumpets.

Now narrowing so much, the quarry can be sealed off with a short wall, which is inset with a heavy, dark wooden door. The path then plunges into the deeper shade of the wilder Quarry, the part extended by Sir Arthur, with its glooms and depths, ivy-clad rock, mosses and ferns. Children love to run and hide in the twisting, turning spaces, amongst the towering rocks that are covered with woodland plants. Beautiful though the Quarry is, it is a wonderful moment to burst out of the dark woods into the bright light and suddenly see the castle, lapped by green fields, under a wide sky.

The garden at Belsay today is a truly sensual experience, alternating between light and shade, coolness and heat, enclosure and openness, the tamed and the wild. There is a real sense of the past, and of the two extraordinary men who created the garden. Despite its vision of the sublime, it is not without its human touches. If you look carefully on the rock face at the start of the Quarry Garden, you can see the names of much-loved pets carved into the wall, Polly, Judy and Mandy; just one of the many elements contributing to the atmosphere of this unique place.

opposite (top): *The Hall rises above* Euphorbia griffithii *'Fireglow' and purple alliums.*
opposite (bottom): *Towering walls of stone frame the Grotto.*
above: *A secret, dark pool is hidden amongst ferns.*
left: *Worth seeking out - pets' names are carved into the rock face.*

Bide-A-Wee Cottage

left: *Tall* Cephalaria gigantea *almost reaches the stone-flagged roof of the shed.*
opposite: *The quarry face itself can be seen to the right of the meandering path.*

FASHIONED OUT OF AN OLD QUARRY, the garden at Bide-A-Wee Cottage nestles in a hollow, scooped out of a windswept hillside that rises above the Font valley. As blustery weather whips up the hill, it is broken first by beech, oak and pine, then by further layers of shelter from birch and holly then finally by an immaculately clipped leylandii hedge. Inside the sculpted bowl of the once quarry, Mark Robson has spent the last twenty-five years creating from scratch a surprisingly lush garden in this wind-battered area of Northumberland.

Now a Chartered Landscape Architect, Mark first started to make a garden here when he was only thirteen. Except for one tree, the land around his parents' stone cottage was completely barren. Whin and scrub grew in the spoil and broken stones of the quarry basin, but the young Mark wanted to make a small pond in the bottom. As his enthusiasm and knowledge grew, so the garden grew from the first plants around the pond's edge to include the dramatic slopes surrounding it.

A quarter of a century later, the garden is justly famous and it is hard to imagine those early days. Tall trees planted on the quarry rim emphasise its depth, narrow paths snake up and down the rock faces or widen into places to sit, whilst a series of pools reflect the wide sky above. It's a cool, verdant space with wildflowers seeding into crevices, cushions of moss between fern-hung rocks and vast leaves of gunnera shading the water.

Arriving at Bide-A-Wee, you walk first down a stone-flagged path through quite the prettiest sales area. Here, plants from his specialist nursery are paid for in a wonderful wooden hut built by Mark and his father using wood from the valley below and glazed with tiny, old glass panes. Of strong construction (the stone-flagged roof weighs four tons) the shed, with its little wood-burning stove looks as if it has been here for many years. A dark arch through a yew hedge gives a glimpse of pale agapanthus as the garden opens out beyond.

From a small lawn surrounded by cottage garden plants, grass paths lead off in different directions like choices in a storybook. All, ultimately, lead down into the quarry, but the tall planting screens it from view. One path is a grassy walk between apple trees, scented in autumn by white phlox and edged with grasses, geraniums, and leafy hostas. This was the ancient spoil ramp where horse and cart would haul stone from the quarry below. Huge pools of *Geranium maccrorhizum* spill out from the side borders, backed by the silvery sea holly Miss Willmott's Ghost and the golden plumes of the grass *Stipa gigantea*.

In spring, the beds below the apple trees are bright with tulips, violas, primulas, and euphorbias. By summer, these borders are carefully colour schemed in a palette of blues, mauves, and whites punctuated with richer reds, whilst autumn is opulent with reds and golds. The final glimpse of the quarry itself is cleverly held back for a moment by a high stone wall until you step through a tall arch.

Tall conifers rise out of the quarry bowl. At its heart are two dark ponds separated by a wooden planked bridge, their contours hidden by huge leaves of gunnera, rodgersia, and skunk cabbage. The pond margins are brightly coloured with primulas in early summer. Although this is a frost pocket, tree ferns enhance the tropical feel and the air of mystery. Emanating from the centre, paths zigzag around the rocky sides, leading up steps partly obscured by miniature cotoneaster or ferns and back up to sweeps of lawn on the ground above.

below: *Pink bistort and rodgersias by the plank bridge.*

right: *The reflecting pool is cradled in the bowl of the old quarry.*

Looking down at the luxuriant mass of foliage, it is hard to believe that very little topsoil has been brought into this garden. Mark has added his own compost as well as farmyard manure, but as the trees and shrubs have grown, they have laid down their own leafmould or pine needles, helping to create humus for the soil. Having said that, it is still desperately thin and there is only a spit's depth before hitting rock.

The star plant of this garden does need some nurturing with humus-rich soil; *Cardiocrinum giganteum* is a giant Himalayan lily growing to three metres in height with enormous white bells that scent the air in mid summer. These exotic-looking bulbs take seven years to flower from seed and look really stunning in their sunken setting. Even in autumn, their large, plump seedpods have style and structure, adding to the sensuality of a garden where water drips quietly into mossy basins and scents hang in the sheltered air.

Rising up out of the quarry, the paths lead again into flat, grassy spaces, edged with generous plantings of perennial plants. The borders are brimful with spiky sea hollies and giant onorpodum thistles, dark purple *Angelica gigas*, large swathes of geraniums and ornamental grasses; cottage planting on a lavish scale. Knapweeds are used extensively, as Mark holds the National Collection of Centaurea. The ground levels out in front of the cottage, now protected enough by twenty-five years of tree growth to have mauve abutilons flourishing against its walls, rosemary, and catmint at its base. Even the lovely agapanthus from South Africa grows happily, thanks to the sandy soil and fast drainage.

From here, glimpses of the landscape hint at the land beyond until you emerge at a wildflower meadow where the Robsons' thirteen bee-hives stand in a line, protected from the south by whispering birches. It is a testament to Mark's dedication, knowledge, and sheer love of gardening that this amazing garden exists at all on this windy hill. His clever use of the terrain makes it appear much larger than it is, with its multiple levels, narrowing and widening paths, vistas and intimate spaces, a complex and beautiful Northumberland garden.

opposite (top): *Conifers provide a strong framework for hardy plants and rhododendrons.*
opposite (below): *Hardy geraniums peep through a pair of wooden chairs.*
right (top): *The interior of the shed.*
right (centre): *Primulas enjoy the moist ground around the pool.*
right (bottom): *One of Bide-A-Wee's many secluded seating areas.*

opposite: *Cottage garden bistort makes an interesting juxtaposition with an exotic tree fern.*
left: *The spectacular trumpets of the giant lily,* Cardiocrinum giganteum.
below: *The Robsons' beehives stand in a field of buttercups.*

Chesters Walled Garden

Visitors to Chesters Walled Garden arrive through leafy woods of mixed beech and yew before seeing the high brick walls of the garden. It is these woods that cradle the walled garden, sheltering and protecting, and give it its special microclimate. I have spent twenty years here, creating a relaxed blend of the formal and informal, the wild, and the cultivated where Mediterranean herbs grow harmoniously alongside British wildflowers.

Back in 1986, the garden had slipped into decline with dilapidated greenhouses and a cocktail of the finest weeds: bindweed, ground elder, enchanter's nightshade and couch grass. In the centre of the garden stood a chimney, over four metres high, a remnant of an underground boiler system, which swayed ominously in high winds. What the garden did have was a wonderful atmosphere, even in its then rather sad state, and so the task of rescuing and transforming began.

The central part of the mansion at Chesters was built in the eighteenth century, with the walled garden being constructed at the same time. In 1891, the architect Norman Shaw added two flanking wings, the west-facing wing having a curved outline with windows recessed behind tall Corinthian columns. A ha-ha allows for uninterrupted views across the grass parks to the gentle sweep of the river North Tyne. Beyond that rises the broad bulk of Warden Hill, on which can be traced the earthworks of its prehistoric hill fort. This is the view to the south visible from inside the walled garden, a view with wide skies often circled by buzzards as they ride the thermals.

Cleverly positioned, the garden takes full advantage of the site with its gentle south-facing slope. The north wall was a 'hot wall' with a flue system to heat it; it was the job of 'stove boys', lads of just ten or eleven, to keep the fires alight all night long. The smoke can clearly be seen in an archive photograph from the late nineteenth century by the prolific Northumbrian photographer, John Pattison Gibson. In Victorian days, there were several large glasshouses capable of producing exotic fruit and flowers for Chesters house, the more mundane vegetables being grown in a second walled garden further away.

In the 1920s, there were still fifteen gardeners employed at Chesters and it was here that Geoffrey Moon, who would later become Head Gardener at Wallington, served his apprenticeship. Like many estate gardens, however, the number of gardeners dwindled and by the 1980s there was just one. I remember my first spring and the task of cutting down all the brown, dead stalks of herbaceous plants left from the previous year and waiting expectantly to see what would emerge from the two acres within the walls.

above: *Ox-eye daisies tumble over the edge of the Mediterranean pond.*
opposite: *Orange daylilies, pink* Epilobium *'Isobel' and yellow* Inula magnificum *create layers of imaginative planting.*

The layout followed a classic pattern, with gravel paths forming a cross shape in the centre and box hedges defining the boundaries of flowerbeds. Together with my partner Kevin, I cleared and weeded, delighted at discovering some very good peonies and a few other interesting plants. One of these was an aster with tall dark stems and sprays of delicate mauve flowers that has only recently been verified as unique and named 'Star of Chesters'. There were two unusual medicinal plants, birthwort and pokeweed, that I like to think may have been used in veterinary medicine on the estate.

Taking the original layout as a guide, one area at a time was redesigned with no initial plan on paper. We simply responded to the quality and atmosphere of each part of the garden, creating new borders, ponds and herb-lined paths. With a specialist nursery at the entrance to the garden, the box-edged beds were filled with display plants, which quickly grew in number after trips to nurseries all over Britain and the addition of plant collections from abroad. The garden, then known as Hexham Herbs, exhibited at Hampton Court Palace Flower Show and BBC Gardeners' World Live.

opposite: A surprisingly hardy tamarisk suns itself behind the flowering Thyme Bank.
left: *The Thyme Bank is a living tapestry of colourful foliage and flowers.*
below: *A glimpse of parkland beyond the walled garden, with gardener's garters grass in the foreground.*

Being right on the line of Hadrian's Wall, and next door to Chesters Roman Fort, the walled garden was ideal for showing the plants that the Romans grew during their occupation of Britain. The site of a Roman road actually runs across the garden from north-west to south-east and the small Roman garden straddles its line. Divided into four square beds; it is a scaled-down version of the type of courtyard garden or peristyle set at the heart of the Roman villa. Two beds are filled with culinary herbs, marjoram, chives, Good King Henry, marsh-mallow and other Roman favourites. One bed holds medicinal plants, whilst the fourth displays sacred herbs such as vervain and violet.

In 1986, the collection of thymes was accepted as a National Collection. The plants are grown on the Thyme Bank, which is held back by large sandstone blocks, knee-high from the ground, giving the good drainage and sunny position that these Mediterranean plants require. Flowering is staggered over two months with the Bank at its height in mid to late June when the mass of spreading and rounded shapes resemble a Persian tapestry of colour and are much loved by bees. The scent is heady and ranges from lemon and orange through culinary thyme to pine resin and camphor.

Flowering after the thymes, the marjorams also attract bees and butterflies and form a second National Collection. These are grown in great drifts by the Mediterranean Pond, a rectangular pool that reflects the sky and is home to frogs, toads, newts and dragonflies. Elsewhere, a circular pool is a favourite drinking spot for the many species of birds that frequent the garden, attracted by hip- and seed-bearing plants as well as plentiful nesting sites. An annual bird count is carried out and is on display to visitors. Red squirrels venture into the garden to raid the nuts in the bird feeder. Organically run for many years, the walled garden has become a haven for wildlife, settling into an equilibrium with no need for human intervention. Pests are controlled by natural predators rather than by chemicals.

In 2001, I took over running the garden on my own and changed the name to Chesters Walled Garden. After twenty years it has matured, softening the formal underlying structure with free-flowing informal planting. Wildflowers mingle with rare perennials, their loose, natural lines creating a relaxed feel in the over-brimming borders. Plants spill over the edge of paths, producing meandering vistas, self-seeders often giving unexpected

top: *One of the ancient espalier apple trees in full pink blossom.*
centre: *Salvia & lady's mantle.*
bottom: *Wildflowers teasel, mullein and St. John's wort mixed with unusual pokeweed and double geraniums - the very essence of planting at Chesters.*
opposite (top): *A Victorian water carrier below an arch of golden hop,* Humulus lupulus 'Aureus'.
opposite (bottom): *Silver mounds of cotton lavender in front of rows of pink lavender and golden yarrow.*

results. Sculptures based on plant forms emerge from amongst wavy ferns and spotted lungwort leaves.

As you move around the garden, it changes from light to shade, from wide to narrow paths, from one atmosphere to another. Ox-eye daisies wave gently by the Mediterranean pool where water lilies luxuriate. An arbour half hidden by wild clematis provides shade on hot days. Red tulips fill the formal beds in spring, followed by the gorgeous purple *Salvia* 'Blue Queen' with lady's mantle, then butterfly-covered sedums, providing nectar in every season. Box-edged borders contain neat rows of organically grown vegetables. Old-fashioned roses scent the air all summer long, the magnificent 'Kiftsgate' rose scrambling into the high tops of a yew tree. Hundred-year-old espalier apple trees are tightly trained in neat shapes. Looking back at the early photographs, I am struck by how bare the garden looked in 1986 compared to how it is today with its lush borders and tumbling roses.

The last remaining glasshouse leans at a steep angle against the north wall, its walkway made of Victorian cast-iron grilles in decorative honeycomb patterns. Unheated in winter, it still provides enough protection to grow the more tender herbs, vibrant lemon verbena, sweet scented myrtle, 'Tuscan Blue' rosemary, pineapple sage and golden bay. A productive grape vine has been trained along most of its length giving welcome shade from the summer sun. When the temperature rises, a small plunge pool for frogs allows these valued natural predators to cool off; often several heads can be seen emerging from the water, dotted by the green spots of pondweed.

Being largely based on perennial planting, growth in the garden progresses through the seasons from ground level to above head height. By autumn, there are large swathes of spiky acanthus, colourful asters, rich burgundy Joe Pye weed and the hemp agrimony on which so many insects love to feed. The extensive collection of Sanguisorba, given full status as a National Collection in 2006, lasts well into the first frosts with a stunning variety of pink, white and wine red bottlebrush flowers, some drooping delicately, some standing upright, whilst 'John Coke' fizzes in crazy patterns like live sparklers. Stems and leaves rustle in the grass garden, jungle-like under their speckled canopy of eucalyptus trees.

With the autumn growth way above head height, the sensation evoked is akin to that of childhood when everything was taller. If there has been one single vision in my design of the walled garden, it has been this: to echo and build on memories of my childhood in a rather wild Berkshire garden. I have achieved this by weaving wildflowers into the borders, by hinting at mysteries down the next path and by allowing many of the herbs to self-seed with abandon. It is the legacy of the past, that rigid structure of paths and box hedges that makes this freedom possible and holds the balance with the 'controlled chaos' of the imaginative planting.

below: *A stunning combination;* Papaver orientale *'Springtime' and the purple leaves of* Lysimachia ciliata *'Firecracker'.*

opposite: *The curious pink spires of pokeweed,* Phytolacca clavigera, *give way to first green, then almost black berries.*

Chillingham Castle

left: *The best views of the parterre are from the upper levels of the castle.* **opposite:** *Mark Wahlinger's sculpture with lady's mantle frothing at its feet.*

FEW GARDENS CAN HAVE such a romantic backdrop as that of Chillingham Castle. Its battlemented towers rise sheer above the lawns and flowerbeds, symbols of strength in the once turbulent Borders. Fought over, besieged and visited by kings, it has stood in this spot since the thirteenth century, when the Grey family first seized the existing single tower. Remarkably, it has been in the hands of the Greys ever since, added to, strengthened and modified over the years.

When Sir Humphrey Wakefield and his wife, Katherine, daughter of Lady Mary Grey of nearby Howick Hall, bought Chillingham, it had been left roofless and floorless since 1933, its rooms filled with four feet of pigeon manure. The garden had been similarly abandoned, the once neat box hedges shapeless and overgrown, with brambles making the paths impassable. Restoring the castle as a family home has taken some twenty-five years but it has been done so sympathetically that the antiques, tapestries, armour and furnishings look as if they have been acquired over generations.

It is the same with the garden, which, thanks to Lady Wakefield's interest in plants, appears to have the settled nature of a much older design. In fact, in the 1920s, the borders were formally laid out with sparser plantings of tender bedding and not the dreamy, soft herbaceous plants of today. Known as the Italian garden, the glorious parterre lies to the west of the castle and was designed by the Royal architect, Sir Jeffrey Wyatville who redesigned much of Windsor Castle and Chatsworth. He was commissioned in 1828 to alter the grounds and gardens of Chillingham, which he did by creating avenues and vistas, lodges and park gates, as well as the swirling patterns of the parterre.

The topiary shapes are created by sturdy 'walls' of yew which echo the castle stronghold, with lower, gentler hedges of box below them. Unusually, the yew hedges slope outwards towards the top, sometimes giving the effect of the oncoming prow of a ship. There are round finials atop the yew or great domes of the golden variety that rest on the lawns like giant tea cosies. The space between yew and box is filled in with skirts of lavender, softening the geometry of the repeated shapes. Stone urns sit in the middle of circles of lawn and a fountain marks the centre of the parterre. This, along with all the other statues and embellishments were added to the previously neglected garden by Sir Humphrey.

Sir Jeffrey's design can best be appreciated from the top of a flight of stone steps by the castle. Parterres were designed to be seen from the upper floors of a house, so it is from above that the complexity of the design is revealed. Wave shapes are made by the curling double lines of box that have only a few inches gap between them. Two pretty beds of pale pink Felicity roses are underplanted with the hazy, blue catmint, Six Hills Giant, and the border immediately below the castle walls is planted with white flowers highlighted with pink.

A long crenellated wall stretches around the Italian garden and it is below this that Lady Wakefield has created the longest herbaceous border in Northumberland. Having cleared the jungle and brambles, she was given plants by her sister at Bramdean garden in Hampshire and these provided a framework for this huge border. Colours and shapes are repeated along its length, giving it a linear unity; blues predominate early in the year, followed by a careful composition of pink, purple and blue, then yellow and red leading to the hotter colours of the autumn.

In June, intense splashes of magenta *Geranium psilostemum* define the border at intervals, softened by creamy astrantias, blue greater bellflowers, tradescantias, knapweeds and lupins. Large glaucous-leaved hostas add their strong foliage, and heavy sprays of peonies lean against the box hedge. July is dominated by tall yellow *Inula magnifica*, with startling, red lychnis, crimson spikes of *Polygonum amplexicaule*, toned down by creamy plumes of goat's beard. As the summer lengthens, there are lavender-blue flowers of *Verbena bonariense* in front of imposing stands of purple Joe Pye weed and bronze fennel.

left (top): *The pretty daisy,* Erigeron karvinskianus, *grows in cracks in the stone steps.*

left (centre): *The parterre viewed from the jousting grandstand.*

left (bottom): *Magenta* Geranium psilostemum *is planted at intervals down the long herbaceous border.*

opposite (top): *Pale pink Felicity roses soften this view of the Border stronghold.*

opposite (bottom): *A lion's head fountain at the centre of the parterre.*

At the far end of the herbaceous border there is a large Victorian rockery thickly covered in native ferns, with behind it a massive, fifteen-foot thick wall that was once a grandstand for jousting tournaments. The marble Christ figure that stands above the rockery is a sculpture by Mark Wahlinger entitled *Ecco Homo* and was one of a series of conceptual works of art placed on the empty plinth in Trafalgar Square and brought here by the Wakefields in 2002. Other recent additions are the square pool set in the south lawn and the cannons that point to the skyline, seemingly defending the castle.

Tall wellingtonia trees edge the lawn and a path leads off into a network of woodland walks that twist alongside a burn until reaching its source at an ornamental lake. The sense of history is tangible, the castle standing defiant in its wooded demesne, but it is the restoration of the garden that adds a gentler, more domestic dimension.

opposite: *Neptune surveys the garden from below a scallop shell.*
left: *A narrow slit runs down the middle of this scroll of box.*
below: *The castle seen from the far end of the parterre where Ecco Homo stands.*

Cragside

WHEN LORD ARMSTRONG decided to build Cragside on a rocky, bare hillside above the village of Rothbury, he chose a suitably dramatic spot where the house could dominate the wild landscape. Designed by the architect Norman Shaw and completed in 1866, the imposing building with its tall chimneys and steep tower needed an equally sublime setting. This was a time when plant hunters were travelling into remote regions bringing back romantic descriptions of the places they had seen. Lord Armstrong, inspired by Sir Joseph Hooker's *Himalayan Journals* he envisioned a Himalayan valley with stately conifers and massed rhododendrons leading the eye up to the house on its crag.

What was a bare, scrubby moorland hillside would become, over the years, a densely forested estate of a thousand acres and the view of Armstrong's mansion, seen rising above the Iron Bridge, a well-known image. Everything was executed on a large scale, from the importing of tons of topsoil to the huge sandstone boulders that make up the Rock Garden in front of the house. In line with the fashion of the time, it was laid out to suggest natural strata amongst which could be grown alpine flowers and low shrubs. Over the years, *Rhododendron ponticum* and other invasive plants had taken it over, so the National Trust, who now own Cragside, began clearing this in 1988, replanting with heathers and azaleas, and alpine plants in the rocky crevices, and reinstating its cascade. This is a Victorian rockery on a truly spectacular scale.

Behind the house, the ground rises steeply, crisscrossed by many interconnecting paths that wind their way up and down amongst trees and rocks. The most spectacular time of year here is in June when the rhododendrons are in full flower and the hillside is transformed by purple, mauve, and red, just like the Himalayan forest that inspired it. The dazzling colours are reflected in the still, dark waters of the twin lakes of Nelly's Moss high up on the hill and a drive through the estate at this time of the year is a memorable experience.

Below the house, the land shelves down to the Debdon burn with its famous Iron Bridge, and under the many magnificent trees that soar upwards in the little valley there are paths worth exploring. These eventually lead up to the Formal Garden, which occupies a series of sunny terraces on richer alluvial soil than that of the area surrounding the house. Although a range of winter glasshouses were lost in the 1920s, this is still a prime example of a Victorian garden in its heyday with carpet bedding, bulbs and dahlias, formality and precision. It is watched over by the pretty, pointed clock tower that chimes the hours from its wooded knoll.

After the sombre shade of the woods, the view from the Formal Garden is expansive, the skyline dark with the brooding outline of the Simonside Hills.

opposite: *Cragside House on its rocky outcrop above the famous iron bridge.*
right: *Vibrant tulips in front of the Orchard House.*
below: *The Dahlia Walk is a riot of colour in autumn.*

As if in defiance of this wild landscape, everything in the garden is controlled and ordered, from the stone-edged lawns and clipped hollies to the magnificent glasshouse and decorative bedding. Each year sees a change of theme in the exuberant carpet bedding, laid out on a long, rectangular sloping bed. Swirling patterns are created from fleshy, grey echevarias, resplendent gold pyrethrums, silver antennarias and pink sedums. Weeding can only be done by kneeling on a wooden board laid across the bed; this is carpet bedding at its very finest.

As the bedding plants cannot be set out until frost-free June, spring is made colourful with many tulips, followed by pansies, polyanthus, forget-me-nots, double daisies and gloriously scented wallflowers. These surround the only remaining glasshouse, the fabulous Orchard House that was specifically designed by Lord Armstrong for producing early fruit. Large grey slabs of stone, their fronts softly curved, surmount terraces within the glasshouse to maximise light. On these are placed Lord Armstrong's intriguing and unique large pots containing fruit trees. So that the tree ripens on every side, each one is set on a turntable, which can be rotated on three cast wheels set in white metal bearings. There are peaches, nectarines, pears, apples, mandarins, lemons, grapefruit and figs - an impressive selection to grow in Northumberland.

opposite: View to the dark profile of the Simonside hills.
above: *Beautiful swirling patterns are created in the carpet bedding.*
right (top): *Carpet bedding at its finest - the theme is changed each year.*
right (centre): *Cragside's spring bedding display.*
right (bottom): *Shadows against the loggia wall.*

Every year in October, Cragside hosts an Apple Day when rows of wicker baskets are filled with produce from the Orchard House, all labelled with evocative or quaint names; 'Knobby Russet', 'Burr Knot', 'Sheep's Nose', 'Devonshire Quarranden', 'Flower of the Town' and 'Beauty of Bath'. Grapes hang plentifully, a sumptuous blue black on their upright poles. Celery and parsley flourish under the glass and scent the whole greenhouse. Autumn is also the time of dahlias, another Victorian passion. There are 700 mixed cultivars planted annually along the Dahlia Walk, a spectacular display for late season that attracts numerous butterflies and bees.

Below the Dahlia Walk, steps lead down to the Italian Terrace, which is also very colourful in autumn. At its centre is the pretty cast-iron Loggia, its white painted, flat arches and glass roof reminiscent of railway architecture. Under its protection, the Loggia is brilliant with pelargonium and fuchsias, its bench a suntrap, delicately striped by shadows from the slender pillars. There is the sound of water splashing from a fountain which plays into a quatrefoil-shaped raised pool. Recently reinstated, its large blocks of stone were found dumped elsewhere on the estate. Rebuilding the pool was part of the National Trust's reconstruction of the Italian Terrace.

above: *Autumn's Apple Day is an annual event.*
below: *A glowing display of apples.*
opposite: *Rhododendrons by the edge of Nelly's Moss lake.*

Lord Armstrong's engineering skills also led him to design the flower beds on the Italian Terrace with six-foot-high glass walls set in wooden frames to give wind protection to the plants. These have recently been rebuilt in white-painted wood, minus the glass, and create a strong framework around the many colourful perennials. It feels rather like peering into a roped-off room, its furnishings richly coloured by purple sedums, glowing penstemons, yellow crocosmias, blue agapanthus, exotic red *Lobelia tupa* and spiky sea hollies. It is remarkable that some of these plants can be grown at this altitude; the same goes for the Moroccan broom and other borderline tender plants that thrive against the Terrace wall.

Above the Orchard House, the Top Terrace used to house the glasshouses that were taken down in the 1920s and, in an echo of the Italian Terrace, their footprint has been replaced with white-painted timber structures. There is the Palm House with its rectangular fish pool and water lilies, clusters of pots containing succulents, grey agaves, palms and exotic scents. The Tropical Fernery is a curious mass of boulders forming walls amongst which are mosses and ferns, with a tall, fringed tree fern, its greenery offset by the red of begonias.

There are even larger boulder walls in the Temperate Fernery and an uneven rock slab path winds under a cool arch. Ferns crowd amongst the rocks, the native hart's tongues enjoying the shade and curling over a tiny green pool but there are also exotics; eucomis, the pineapple plant with its strange flowers, myrtle and the brittle leaves of cycad. The fourth 'building' that gives a flavour of the original is the Show House, which is planted with perennials, many of them at their best in late season. Overlooked by eucalypts, there are some tender plants; strap leaved phormiums, abutilons, petunias and fuchsias surrounding tall buddleias, a magnet for butterflies.

Everywhere is the Victorian command over nature; brilliant bedding fashioned into pictures, Mediterranean fruits tended under glass and the flaunting of often tender plants in this upland area of Northumberland. Perhaps it is the contrast with the rugged landscape and the Simonside Hills that seem to be perpetually in shadow, but this garden seems the height of order over wildness. It is not surprising that Cragside was once described as 'the palace of a modern magician'.

right: *White woodwork provides an unusual framework for the Italian Terrace.*

Dawyck Botanic Garden

THERE ARE FOUR GARDENS that comprise the National Botanic Gardens of Scotland: the Royal Botanic Garden Edinburgh and Benmore, Logan and Dawyck Botanic Gardens. Each has a different climate allowing for a range of growing conditions. The arboretum at Dawyck is the coldest, spreading up a steep hillside in the beautiful Tweed valley, where the winter temperature can drop to -22°C. Plants here have to be hardy, and the garden has a worldwide reputation for northern hemisphere trees. As planting began over three hundred years ago, many of them have reached a magnificent height and stature, making this a woodland garden that is wonderful to visit in any season.

Three families shaped the land, transforming it from a bleakly lovely valley by planting shelterbelts in the thin, acidic soil. It began with the Veitches who settled here in the fifteenth century and planted Scotland's first exotic tree species, a European horse chestnut, in 1650. They also introduced the silver fir, *Abies alba*, in 1680; one of these original trees still survives in Heron Wood. The second family was the Naesmyths who took over the estate a few years later, Sir James Naesmyth being a botanist, trained under Linnaeus. He planted some of the first larches in Scotland in company with, if the story is true, the great Swedish botanist himself.

In 1830, the original house at Dawyck was destroyed by fire and the then owner, Sir John Naesmyth, replaced it with a steeply gabled and turreted mansion. Privately owned, it stands on flat ground at the base of the arboretum's steep hill, into which hillside Sir John had cut garden terraces with Italian stonework and ornamental urns. He sponsored plant hunters who were exploring North America, including the Perth born David Douglas who introduced many important trees following his trail up the West Coast of America. Many of these historic trees and shrubs still thrive at Dawyck.

above: *A fiery red acer is dwarfed by a wellingtonia tree.* **opposite:** *The wellingtonia,* Sequioadendron giganteum, *a giant of the tree world.*

As well as planting many acres of trees, Sir John made a lucky discovery when he spotted a beech seedling, which was growing unusually upright. He moved it to a spot near the house where it still grows, its fastigiated form creating a narrow, columnar shape nearly thirty metres high. This has been propagated and distributed across the world under the name of the Dawyck beech. The estate changed hands again in 1897 and was bought by the Balfour family. They also had a great love of trees and added to the collection, again sponsoring plant-hunting expeditions. They underplanted the trees with shrubs, especially rhododendrons, and many thousands of daffodil bulbs.

In 1978, the sixty acres of arboretum were given to the nation by Colonel Balfour to be looked after by the Royal Botanic Garden Edinburgh. Ten years of work was needed to remove dangerous trees, strengthen windbreaks, erect deer fences, and identify, then catalogue, the numerous plants and trees. New paths and vistas were opened up and the garden was opened to the public. Becoming a National Botanic Garden, the garden could be added to with new wild collected plants and is ever expanding. The present Curator, David Knott, has run Dawyck for 14 years. Unlike most gardens, he has to plan for the long term, imagining how something will look in fifty or a hundred years' time.

Although the arboretum is a scientific 'museum' of plants with many specialist collections, it has great charm and atmosphere. Everything is labelled, but this does not detract from the natural beauty of the woodland setting. The Scrape Burn comes tumbling down the hillside forging a narrow glen with paths that crisscross over bridges. Snowdrops line the Burn, followed by the large, fleshy leaves of skunk cabbage and the huge umbrellas of gunnera, which just survives the cold winters. In June, there are

right (top): *Ferns surround an Italianate urn.*
right (centre): *Perennials line the stream by the Swiss Bridge*
right (bottom): *Italianate steps on the Azalea Terrace.*
opposite: *Ferns do well in Dawyck's cool climate.*

fabulous swathes of meconopsis, blue Himalayan poppies that revel in the humus-rich, lime free soil and delight visitors with their vivid blue petals.

In recent years, drifts of herbaceous perennials have been planted in the 'core' area of the Burn to give colour under the green canopy of the trees in the summer; rodgersias, astilbes, hostas and other plants that like cool, rich soil and can look after themselves. There is the constant sound of water from the stream as the path winds its way up the steep slopes and across the pretty Swiss Bridge. Wildflowers have sprung up in the long grass, thanks to a change in management routine, with just a single cut in July. Ox-eye daisies, cowslips, and primroses are happy in the woodland grasses, whilst long dormant seed of the common spotted orchid, *Dactylorhiza fuchsii*, has re-awakened.

above: *Meconopsis lit up by late afternoon sun.*
opposite: *Acer leaves in autumn.*

As education and conservation are a priority at Dawyck, there are several trails for visitors. Using a leaflet, the Rare Plant Trail can be followed in treasure hunt fashion leading to Scottish native plants growing amongst grasses and rocks. In a damp spot, the glorious globeflower lifts its yellow cups to the sun, growing as abundantly here as it once did in water meadows. The maiden pink is another rarity that grows in thin soil where it is not outcompeted by tall grasses.

With so many of Dawyck's famous trees being Douglas discoveries, there is a David Douglas Trail. He introduced a staggering two hundred and twenty new plant species to Europe and some of these are highlighted on the Trail. These range from the commonly grown flowering currant, *Ribes sanguineum*, with its red spring flowers, to some of his great trees, noble fir, western hemlock, Sitka spruce and the eponymous Douglas fir.

With wild collected plants constantly being added to this dynamic garden, new areas are always being developed. There are certain core collections such as cotoneaster, berberis, sorbus, rhododendron, and betula and David Knott has himself taken part in expeditions to the Far East. With areas of the arboretum devoted to China, Nepal, America, and Europe, the visitor can see all these plants brought together in a 'Round the World in eighty minutes' tour.

Autumn brings another dimension to Dawyck when the ground under the trees is studded with fungi pushing up through the leaf mould. In the Heron Wood is the world's first Cryptogamic Sanctuary, begun in 1993, where fallen timber is left to rot down and encourage the growth of ferns, horsetails, club mosses, liverworts and fungi. Many of these are microscopic and an incredible ten thousand species have been recorded, making this one of the most scientifically studied areas of the world. It is not unusual to come across a tutor carrying a basket full of wood blewits and false chanterelles.

The fallen leaves of autumn make sumptuous pools under the spreading trees. Luminous acers from Japan are vibrant beneath the enormous ancient conifers. Walking under their shelter is like being in the glow of a heat lamp; red fills up the senses. Colour is equally splendid earlier in the year when the rhododendrons flower and the Azalea Terrace is resplendent with orange, yellow, pink and deep red flowers. However, it is the 'champion' trees that soar high above all these, some of the oldest, rarest, and finest trees in the world. The tallest is *Abies grandis*, a giant fir tree, one of Douglas's plants, now over forty-five metres tall, a truly memorable sight in this Scottish valley garden.

left: *An acer glows in autumn light.*
above: *A summer sky above the Azalea Terrace.*

Floors Castle Garden

THE LARGEST INHABITED CASTLE in Scotland, Floors is the home of the Duke and Duchess of Roxburghe. This magnificent, turreted, honey coloured building stands proudly above the River Tweed, with views from the house of sweeping pastures and parkland trees. Not to interrupt this tranquil scene, the walled garden was situated at a little distance from the house and would once have been highly productive, with trained fruit trees and vegetables. Like many such gardens, it has been put to a new use as a garden centre but creating a square around the working area is a series of simply outstanding herbaceous borders.

Most flower borders are designed for a season-long display but here at Floors, one border comes out after the other, forming a progression around the garden. This begins with a carefully planned late spring border in fresh colours of blue, white, and yellow, then moves through a summer border of warmer tones before culminating in a stupendous autumn border that drenches the senses with brilliant hot colour. It is not surprising that this incredible display should have taken many years to perfect and it is indeed the result of fifty years work by Billy Crozier who, after gardening for this length of time at Floors, retired in 2006.

Billy began work in the gardens at Floors after he left school at the age of fifteen, becoming Head Gardener in 1984. He has witnessed many changes in the garden, from the days when it was private, save for an afternoon a week when locals from Kelso could visit, to the busy café, deli, and garden centre of today. Fashions in gardening have similarly changed over the years; in 2003, a pair of traditional Scottish borders were taken out and replaced by the 'hot' borders, with dahlias making a comeback. The plants matured quickly, thanks to the enriched soil and Billy's lifetime of experience in gardening. He could look out daily and see the borders he created from the crenellated Gardener's Cottage, swagged in Virginia creeper. Retiring to a cottage on the estate, his work is continued by Andrew Simmons who was Head Gardener at Balmoral.

The 'hot' borders are superb; eye-smacking colour, awash with scents and butterflies, a total sensual experience. Carmine cannas luxuriate with tropical purple foliage, jostling with red lobelias and nicotiana, dwarf orange-red dahlias, flaming crocosmias, purple red knautia and dusky sedums. Deep purple fennel has feathery foliage

opposite: The crenellated Gardener's Cottage looks onto the 'hot' border.
below: *Billy Crozier working in the border in September.*

at the back, maroon Joe Pye weed attracts late-season insects, and bright yellow marjorams and yellow geums light up the front. There are many types of dahlia, varying in height, some with dark purple foliage, as well as the tender and curiously scented chocolate cosmos.

At the other end of the colour spectrum, the late spring border is freshly bright with blue, gold, and cream. Lime green lady's mantle tumbles onto the edge of the gravel path, swathes of vivid yellow loosestrife rising above it with, above that, the tall creamy plumes of goat's beard. There are many shades of blue, including indigo delphiniums, ice-blue campanulas, grey-blue leaves of hostas, and mauve-blue spikes of catmint. Stately spires of foxtail lilies light up the back of the borders and blowsy pink peonies open their full cups to visiting bees. It is a masterpiece of carefully graduated colours and repeated shapes.

The summer border becomes warmer in tone, with annuals bedded out at the front; there are deep purple-or-

above: *Magenta Geranium psilostemum with blue delphiniums.*
opposite: *Swags of red roses back the summer border.*
previous page: *Lady's mantle, campanulas and goat's beard in the early summer border.*

green-flowered nicotianas, fluffy cosmos, and blue ageratums. Poisonous monkshood is a deep shade of blue, contrasting with the rich gold of tall plants of yarrow. Warm yellow also comes from drifts of golden rod, offset by petrol blue globe thistles and the delicate feathery heads of thalictrum. All along the back of the borders, the red roses American Pillar and Dorothy Perkins hang in great swags along rusted chains.

There is room for vegetables here too; red and yellow veined chard, lusty green spinach, red lettuces, courgettes, and fat heads of artichoke. Regularly spaced fruit trees have tightly pruned spurs; strawberries are netted against the birds and runner beans twine up bamboo canes. Plums ripen against the warm brick walls, behind a long bed entirely planted with different varieties of phlox. Just across the path is a border composed of intense red peonies; there is space enough here to devote borders to a single type of plant, a stunning arrangement as in the huge stand of silvery *Onopordum acanthium*, often known as the Scotch thistle.

The walled garden is the principal attraction at Floors, but there are some other delights. Beneath an arch in the garden's brick wall, a peep through a blue-painted, barred gate gives a glimpse of the box parterre planted to commemorate the millennium. It features the linked initials of the Duke and Duchess; G, V, and R scrolled in extravagant swirling letters on what is known as the Queen's lawn. Inspired by a similar design used on Floors Castle linen in 1900, the parterre was commissioned from James Marshall, former Gardens Advisor to the National Trust. There is a central ducal coronet created from euonymus and an M in box plants for the year 2000.

Creating the parterre was a huge undertaking, involving the importation of a thousand tonnes of topsoil and a hundred tonnes of gravel and stone. It can be viewed from a level terrace above the Queen's lawn where it is easiest to see the huge letter shapes, which end with a flourish in decorative box balls. A calm, green space for most of the year, the millennium parterre is backed by a large rectangle of rhododendrons, which burst into colour in July.

From here, a walk beneath stately trees, leads to the wide, lawned areas in front of the imposing castle. Apart from two flower borders hard by the castle walls and a pretty, formal courtyard full of yellow roses, there is no garden as such. This allows for splendid, uninterrupted views of gently sloping fields, solitary trees, and small copses, with the wide River Tweed beyond. It forms a classic eighteenth century landscape, an equally beautiful contrast to the rich, vibrant colours of the magnificent walled garden.

right: *Crocosmias and dahlias join the riot of colour in the 'hot' border.*
opposite: *Spikes of yellow loosestrife and delphiniums lead the eye up to swags of roses.*

National Collections and the National Council for the Conservation of Plants and Gardens

SEVERAL OF THE GARDENS in this book have National Collections; there are six hundred and fifty registered collections in Britain and they form the basis of the conservation strategy of the NCCPG the National Council for the Conservation of Plants and Gardens.
Collection holders have knowledge and expertise about their particular group of plants. You can join the organisation, which has local talks, plant sales and other activities as an ordinary member.

Halls of Heddon

AFTER SOME YEARS of being rather out of fashion, dahlias have come back into vogue, and appear in planting schemes once more. This must be welcomed by the family-run nursery of Halls of Heddon, which has continued to propagate and grow huge numbers of both dahlias and chrysanthemums over the years. The showfields at West Heddon are open to the public from late August until the first frosts and are a truly stunning sight.

The layout is utilitarian; car park, garden centre, glasshouses are all functional areas from necessity. The plants themselves are grown in long rows, in a down-to-earth, no frills kind of way, but when they are all flowering at once, it is quite amazing. Wander at will through row upon row of waist- or head-high blooms, marvelling at the sheer variety of colours, forms, and foliage types.

Individual varieties are allocated strips, seven metres in length, each clearly labelled with style, colour and height. The names alone are evocative: Carolina Moon, Kenora Sunset, Allan Snowfire. Stout stakes at the end of each section support a strong, square mesh laid horizontally, through which the plants are grown. The wire can hardly be seen, hidden by the profusion of colour and foliage. Butterflies dance in and out of the exotic rows; blooms are crowded with red admirals and bumblebees. The dahlia leaves glisten with dew, backlit by autumn sunshine, which turns some petals translucent. The myriad flowers are jewel colours in paint box strips.

Visitors search the colourful rows, taking notes of the dahlias that they would like to grow. These are then ordered and can be bought as tubers in winter or young plants in spring. The catalogue list is comprehensive, with notes of the plants' suitability for exhibition, cut flower or garden growing. They are divided into categories such as cactus, decorative, waterlily or

above: *Giant and large flowered dahlias can have blooms that are easily 25cm across.*
opposite: *The giant decorative dahlia 'Jocondo' has large reddish purple flowers.*

collerette, the blooms varying in size from ten centimetres to a whopping twenty-five centimetres. These are the giant cactus types so beloved of show enthusiasts, with heavy, plate-sized flowers and are a world away from the more delicate pompon varieties.

Halls have been growing dahlias since 1921, when William Hall, having been wounded in the First World War, leased the derelict two-acre garden attached to Heddon House. Advised by his doctor to work outdoors, he faced the enormous task of tackling the seriously neglected land and tumbledown greenhouses. Aided by his brother, who would travel over twenty-seven kilometres by bus and on foot on his only day off from his job on the railway, he began in a small way with a general nursery. During the Depression years, William's children, Will, Rita, and Tom, helped after school and at weekends, their dad hawking plants around local villages with a pony and cart.

From early on, William realised the importance of specialisation and the first dahlia and chrysanthemum catalogue was issued in 1931. Being out in the country, he took plants to the market in Newcastle as well as starting a small mail order business. As this grew, he needed more land and brought a ten-acre field at Ovington, putting up glasshouses, which would be run as a nursery by his son Tom. For the next few years, they exhibited their plants at shows, winning a number of medals.

The Second World War brought an abrupt end to expanding fame. Having joined the RAF, Will's plane was shot down over Holland in 1941. The land had to be given over to vegetable production, the only space allowed for non-food crops being a limited amount between the rows of vegetables. By the end of the war in 1945, many varieties had been lost. Stan Hall, the youngest son, had now joined the business and everyone was keen to grow flowers once more. Dahlia stocks were built up again, trials undertaken, shows attended and the business could expand anew.

left (top): *Dahlia fields with the dark red foliage of 'Fire Mountain' in the foreground.*
left (centre): *The superb full bodied red of Dahlia 'Kenora Valentine'.*
left (bottom): *Colour as far as the eye can see beyond the purple foliaged Dahlia 'David Howard'.*

Since that time, the family firm has gone from strength to strength, exhibiting at many shows annually, promoting dahlias and chrysanthemums, and drawing in more family members, with Stan's son and daughter, David and Judith, as well as Tom's daughter, Maxine, joining in. Between the two garden centres, Heddon and Ovington, they sell trees, shrubs and perennials, but it is for their breeding and exhibiting of dahlias that they are world-famous. Tubers are sent out by mail order as far as Australia, New Zealand, and America. Each year they grow well over a hundred thousand plants of dahlias and chrysanthemums combined and since the early days in 1933 they have won many gold medals.

below: Miniature
Decorative Dahlia
Barberry Bluebird.

The showfields at Heddon, such a brilliant sight in autumn, are trial grounds for new varieties. If they prove good, they are listed in the next year's catalogue and there are plants on trial from other countries,

such as New Zealand. Dark-foliaged plants, such as Bishop of Llandaff, are currently in vogue, a deep scintillating red flower set against purple black leaves. The names reflect the drama of the plants. Zorro's flowers are bright blood red and huge. Fire Mountain is the colour of lava with black foliage. The tall Spartacus is a dark red, Black Monarch crimson with black shading. There are plenty of delicate shades too; Shandy is an apricot bronze, good for flower arranging, Golden Amber the colour of honey and Barton Memory a soft salmon.

At the end of the long rows of dahlias, there are three crosswise lines of chrysanthemums. These have the subtler, autumn shades of dusky golds, soft pinks, creams, white and apricots on scented foliage reminiscent of harvest festivals. There are spray chrysanthemums for cutting, in hues of apricot, pink, and burnt orange and intermediate chrysanthemums with large, false-looking globe heads. Biggest of all are the exhibition plants with reflexed petals. Together with the giant dahlias, these are the kind seen in horticultural marquees and staked out in precision rows in the back gardens of enthusiasts.

Dependent on the weather, the trial grounds may only be open for a few weeks but are a vibrant sight amongst the autumn fields. Blackbirds hop about between the brilliantly coloured rows and the restless insects gather late-season nectar from the many flowers. Even the vast compost heap is multicoloured with spent blooms, as deadheading keeps the plants healthy and attractive. It's a very changed scene from the overgrown neglected garden that William Hall first worked on in 1921.

below: Dahlias are good for attracting butterflies - this one is the collerette 'Pooh'.
opposite: Collerette dahlias 'April Heather', 'Fairfield Frost' and 'Pooh' make excellent border plants.
overleaf: The popular dark leaved 'Bishop of Llandaff' is seen here with the white collerette dahlia 'Fairfield Frost' behind.

Herterton House

Hᴇʀᴛᴇʀᴛᴏɴ ɪs ᴀɴ ᴇxᴄᴇᴘᴛɪᴏɴᴀʟ small garden, jewel-like in its colour and precision, created over the last thirty years by Frank and Marjorie Lawley. It has been developed around an old farmhouse and lies next to the rugged, sixteenth-century Bastle house of Hartington. When the Lawleys began to reclaim the garden from its derelict state, they decided not to make a period piece but to experiment with new ideas in design. What they have made is informed by their extensive knowledge of unusual plants and fascination with colour theory; it is a scintillating gem of a garden.

The south-facing front garden is formal with immaculately clipped topiary of yew, holly, box, and ivy. Yew buttresses seem to support the walls of the long low farmhouse. Rows of simple squares of box contain the golden variety, dome-shaped like bee skeps, their skirts frilled with dicentra. These minimal structural elements give an aura of calm and timelessness, further enhanced by the view of serene meadows between which the little Hart Burn runs.

above: *Topiary and stone pots provide balance and symmetry.*
opposite: *The projecting window bay of the house inspired its mirror image in the gazebo.*

A narrow passage, with climbing hydrangea hugging the house wall, leads to a small courtyard Physic Garden bounded on the north by the old granary building. Its round arches, though a typical Northumberland feature, give a flavour of Italian arcade with their cool depths. There are two old wooden benches, softened and faded to grey, tendrils of ivy lapping round statues and swallows nesting on the rafters above. Central to the Physic Garden is a fine, willow-leaved pear, clipped to a cone-headed shape, which recalls the granary arches, as do the repeated patterns of the herb beds themselves.

These are neatly edged in dwarf pink London Pride or white thrift and contain many of the herbs that were used in the Northumberland countryside. The colours are cool and quiet; white goat's rue, silvery wormwood, tiny-flowered vervain, perennial borage, shell-pink marshmallow, and white marjoram. Plants of thyme are grown in simple, round pots. Symmetrically paired beds of the old roses Tuscany and Rosa Mundi are cleverly edged in variegated ground elder.

The larger Flower Garden lies to the north of the house. This too has a strong element of topiary, giving it an underlying structure that it is prominent in winter, less obvious in summer. The Lawleys have drawn on many influences here, understanding of which gives another layer of meaning to the garden. The geometric beds are colour graded, and hint at the passage of time throughout the day. Those nearest the house echo the colours of dawn: delicate pinks, yellows, creams, and whites. Beyond these, the beds are vibrant with orange and blue, reminiscent of the sun at its zenith in a cloudless sky. Lastly, come the violent colours of sunset, reds, blacks, and deep purples with cooler blues and silvers to either side.

below: *A fine willow-leaved pear makes a formal centrepiece in the Physic Garden.*
opposite (top): *Massed orange poppies symbolise the fiery midday sun.*
opposite (centre): *Rich blue geraniums imply the summer skies around the orange of the sun.*
opposite (bottom): *Many shades of green and yellow form the Topiary Garden.*

This is a thoughtful approach to making a garden, one that reflects not just the influence of time on a single day but also on our lives. Coupled with these ideas are the colour theories of two great twentieth-century painters, Klee and Mondrian, and the flowerbeds also make up 'magic square' compositions. In addition, the selection of plants illustrates how flowers came to be chosen for the garden, from pretty natives brought in from fields and hedgerows to curiosities, doubles and coloured-leaved forms that were noticed and treasured.

Knowing what has informed this garden gives it an unusual depth, but it is not necessary to know this to appreciate what is, quite simply, very beautiful. On a warm summer's day, the wind just stirs the tall trees that with holly and shrubs shelter the garden. Sparrows twitter on the house roof above the stone slabbed terrace, which is edged with ferns, violets, *Viola labradorica*, and neatly trimmed ivies. Columnar yew trees stand like Roman pillars with periwinkles at their base. There is calm and order from the gentle early morning colours of pink yarrow, *Achillea* 'The Pearl', silver leaved mullein, violas and golden rod.

Moving away from the shade of the building, the hues are more intense; there are many different blues from agapanthus, sea holly, annual cornflowers, Jacob's ladder, gentian, and salvias. Bright calendula marigolds, orange Peruvian lilies and, that cottage garden stalwart, fox and cubs mimic the hot sun. The sunset finale is set in an enclosure of above-waist-high box with a central stone ornament. There are crimson poppies, deep-coloured scabious, ruby yarrow, bergamot, red cornflowers and the sumptuous spikes of *Sanguisorba sitchensis*, a lovely burnet with burgundy bottlebrushes on tall stems. Outside the box square, the colours drain away as the sky does towards the horizon. Gentleness comes from silver Artemisia, bellflowers, white toadflax and catmint.

A tall yew hedge is the Flower Garden's northern boundary and an archway in its centre gives a glimpse of a complete change in tone. This is the Fancy Garden, a formal parterre of young box plants laid out with precision against fine gravel. Clipped yews surround it and there is a wide stone basin at its

middle on a low plinth. The centre of each of the four parterre beds is crowned by a mushroom-shaped staddle stone and beyond the maze of box hedges stands a tall, thin gazebo. Designed as a viewpoint for the garden as well as the surrounding fields, it mirrors the central part of the house that can be seen from its windows. Two delightful twisted pillars support the roof of a cool alcove and stone steps lead to the upstairs room.

Frank Lawley describes the gazebo as a 'twentieth-century collage', a bit of fun made up of local stone, seventeenth-century Welsh

windows, the twisted pillars bought from a friend and the heavy black door with its knocker. Inside is an exhibition of Marjorie's original drawings for the garden. Wonderfully executed in clear black lines, the names of the plants form decorative blocks; they are text as topiary. They illustrate that this remarkable garden has had an enormous amount of thought and care put into its design; unique can be an overworked word, but here it is quite simply true.

opposite: The gazebo provides a viewpoint over the Fancy Garden.
above: *Sea Holly in the flower garden.*
below: *Benches in the old Granary.*

right: *These little gems for sale are not pot-grown, an unusual method that works.*
below: *Hot-coloured geums and poppies surround this old stone basin.*
opposite: *White spires of flowers on the beautiful St. Bernard's Lily, Anthericum liliago.*

Howick Hall

THE SHELTERED GARDEN of Howick Hall lies in a wooded dip in the land near the fishing village of Craster, famous for its oak-smoked kippers. Up and down the wild coastline, castles hug the rock and the North Sea shapes the sweeping bays, but here at Howick is the kind of microclimate more common on the warmer west coast. An unexpected treasury of rare and sometimes tender plants flourish here thanks to a long tradition of imaginative tree planting.

Howick Hall has been the home of the Grey family since it was built in 1782 and it was the second Earl Grey, Prime Minister and inspiration for the bergamot-scented tea, who planted many of the hardwoods that protect the garden today. Successive members of the family added new layers of shelter, enabling the planting of an understorey of azaleas, camellias, magnolias and other specimen shrubs. When the estate passed to Lady Mary Howick, she enlivened the woodland floor with a mix of blue Himalayan poppies, trilliums, hellebores and primulas, creating drifts of foliage and flower that sparkle beneath the trees.

It is these layers of clever planting that give the garden at Howick its charm. Magnificent trees stand tall against the sea winds, flowering shrubs scent the woodland glades, and perennials luxuriate in the richness of the soil. Nor does it stand still, for the present Lord Howick is a much-respected present-day plant hunter whose travels abroad have enabled him to create an extensive arboretum based almost entirely on wild collected seed.

above: *Daffodil time at Howick Hall.*
opposite: *Special snowdrop walk weekends are announced in the local press.*

At the heart of the garden stands the eighteenth-century house, empty since 1967 because of its size; the family live in an adjoining wing. Although largely uninhabited, the house does not feel ghostly or threatening. Instead, it adds to the calm and dreamy atmosphere of the garden, which is delightfully free of commercialism. This is very much a place for garden-lovers and it is only recently that a charmingly old-fashioned tea room has been opened.

Shallow terraces drop down from the Hall to a meadow by the Howick Burn where trout hide in the shadow of huge gunnera leaves. In spring, the grass is spotted with snake's head fritillaries and deep purple tulips; in autumn, it is the turn of colchicums where late bees dip into chalices of purple and white. These lovely autumn crocuses drift everywhere, there open cups swaying gently under the red of Japanese maples or appearing luminous in the shade of beech trees.

Edged by stone balustrades, the top terrace is a wide gravelled space where aromatic mounds of herbs are allowed to self-seed. Little ferns

and autumn cyclamen grow in cracks in the descending stone steps, adding to the air of informality. In summer, the terrace is bordered by a long, hazy line of blue catmint; by autumn it is fringed with azure agapanthus, these being some of the original plants introduced from South Africa. In the terrace below, a round fishpond is encircled by yew hedges, echoed nearby by a second hedged circle containing red-hot pokers, their colour brilliant against the dark green of the yew.

Large lavender hedges soften the edge of the bottom terrace whilst in the distance, grey willows frame a glimpse of a field grazed by sheep. The bell tower of the little Victorian church peeps out from the trees. There is the sound of water falling in the wood and an occasional chime from the clock on the east wing. Full of scent, sound, and colour, the garden at Howick has a timeless quality, with the ever-present feeling that of the sea is just nearby.

From the meadow in front of the house, the Howick Burn runs below the woodland garden and on through the Long Walk before

entering the sea at a quiet cove strewn with seaweed. Many of the trees and shrubs were given to Lord Howick's grandparents for their silver wedding in the 1930s, and sheltered dells have recently been created so that new introductions from China can be planted. It was here that the official opening of the Howick Arboretum took place in May 2006, the occasion being marked by the planting of a Chinese wingnut tree by the noted plantsman and writer, Roy Lancaster.

Lord Howick has taken part in numerous plant hunting expeditions to remote parts of the world, alongside experts from the Royal Botanic Gardens of both Kew and Edinburgh. Legitimately collected seed is germinated and grown on at Howick until it can be planted out in the ever-expanding Arboretum. Stretching over sixty acres, this contains over eleven thousand trees and shrubs making it one of the finest collections of wild collected trees in Europe and a safe haven for endangered plants.

It is not only new trees that are added to the collection; behind the house a bog garden is constantly being added to with new herbaceous plants brought back from abroad. Lord Howick collects wild seed of asters, aconites, sages and lobelias, trialling these introductions in his Northumbrian garden. The bog garden spreads out from the margins of a large pond; the effect is very natural, with tall primulas growing amongst irises, and huge white lilies opening their trumpets for foraging bees.

In autumn, the specimen trees give a brilliant display of colour. There are vivid reds and purples from the many acers, contrasting with shades of yellow from the graceful cercidiphyllums that edge the sides of the drive. The falling leaves add to the richness of the soil and the tall trees once again provide protection from the buffeting of the sea winds, sheltering this very special garden from the winter storms.

opposite: *Springtime at Howick Hall.*
right (top): *The dark green of this yew circle is the ideal foil for sizzling red-hot pokers.*
right (centre): *Each tree in the arboretum is labelled and recorded on a database.*
right (bottom): *Drifts of autumn crocus, Colchicum autumnale, echo the tulips of spring.*

99

left: *Tulips and narcissus in meadow grasses in spring - a glorious flowery mead.*
top: *Colchicums beneath glowing* Cercidiphyllum japonicum *trees.*
above: *Beech leaves floating in the autumn stream.*

Kailzie

THERE ARE TWO DISTINCT STYLES of garden at Kailzie, the refined, semi-formal Walled Garden, and the wild Woodland Garden that flows naturally around it. Nestling in a wooded glen near Peebles, the views from Kailzie are stunning, looking north to the high, sculpted hills that enclose the magnificent Tweed valley. The Georgian house that once stood here was pulled down in 1962, leaving behind the stable block, fragments of the original tree planting and the large walled garden. The walled garden had been grassed over during the 1939-45 war and so presented a blank canvas to Angela, Lady Buchan-Hepburn, owner and creator of Kailzie Gardens.

Although sheltered by high walls, it presented quite a challenge, tilted as it is to the north and east. The frost here bites deep, with a recording one winter of a destructive minus twenty-four degrees. There have been records of frost in every month of the year, even once on a Midsummer's Day, so, to do well, all the plants have to be very tough. It is a fascinating demonstration of hardiness, for if a plant can grow at

Kailzie, it can grow almost anywhere. Even so, the unheated greenhouses are awash with exotic, summer colour from the many bright fuchsias and pelargoniums.

The high outside of the Walled Garden does in fact feel rather like a protective castle wall. In early June, the tiny fairy foxglove, *Erinus alpinus*, growing abundantly in cracks in the mortar, sports pretty, purple flowers, making the stones spring to life. Roses fan out against the wall, the long thin bed at its base a pattern of alternating hostas, lady's mantle, and catmint. An undulating rhythm is created between the fluted hosta leaves and the contrasting, softer foliage. An iron gate set into the wall gives a peep into the interior of the garden.

Once through the gate, the vista is across immaculate lawns to the white-painted

above: *The laburnum walk is underplanted with catmint, lady's mantle and alliums.*
opposite: *An arbour shades a statue of Mercury in the centre of the Rose Garden.*

greenhouses on the far side. This was the first area that Lady Buchan-Hepburn embarked upon and has swirling island beds with conifers for height, graded down through shrubs to perennials and bulbs. The cool bed shaded by the east wall has large drifts of hostas and astilbes overhung by magnolias. At the centre of the lawn is a stone sundial set on low, octagonal plinths, dated 1811, and this makes a hub for the garden, with a view cross-wise to double, flanking herbaceous borders.

These borders, at their height in July and August, are backed by two glowing, copper beech hedges. They lead the eye to a large wrought-iron gate in the north wall, through which can be glimpsed a sparkling fountain. There are some unifying repetitions in the planting, with herbaceous perennials often mirrored in the opposite border. Shrubs of white potentillas define the ends, with whites, pinks, and mauves from greater bellflowers, goat's rue, delphiniums, phlox, and bistort. These are punctuated by the wine red of *Cirsium* thistles and softened with silver artemisias and tumbling catmint.

To either side of the companion beech hedges, there are compartments, each with a different atmosphere. An enclosed rose garden is laid out in formal beds around a central arbour that arches over a statue of Mercury. A cutting and vegetable parterre has wooden-edged raised beds set in gravel; chrysanthemums, sweet peas, and gladioli grow happily next to kohlrabi, leeks, salad leaves and herbs. Running parallel to this is Kailzie's highlight, a glorious laburnum walk forming cascades of golden flowers in June. At the end of this yellow tunnel is a sculpture of Bacchus under a canopy of silvery willow-leaved pear.

Behind the laburnum walk is a calm little parterre of box diamonds surrounding box cones with white potentillas at intervals alongside. It is a shady, cool green space and very charming, which is repeated on the other side of the vegetable garden next to a tunnel of apple trees trained over wide metal hoops, an echo of the laburnum walk. It is these recurrent shapes and plantings that give the garden cohesion whilst being divided up into different 'rooms'.

right: *An acer is illuminated by glorious autumn sunlight.*

The series of Victorian greenhouses have the original staging and criss-cross iron grating in the floor. Jasmine, solanum, and fig are splayed out against the white walls, and arum lilies open their white trumpets in a moist, redundant trough. The roof of the central span is draped in scented wisteria, the back wall an unusual, curved apse shape where Mediterranean plants stand in large terracotta pots.

Outside the Walled Garden, the large fountain plays noisily into a wide basin, light reflected on the underside of its double bowls. It is surrounded in May by the heady scent of yellow azaleas, stems silver with lichens due to the pure air. Above stands the impressive Kailzie larch, possibly the oldest in Scotland, dating from 1725. From here, the burn tumbles down through daffodil woods, which later are carpeted in bluebells, its banksides thickly planted with gunnera and the vivid magenta *Primula pulverulenta*. Blue meconopsis thrive in peaty beds and a green curved bridge gently spans the stream.

A short detour from the burnside walk leads to a little summerhouse in the wood and the start of the Major's Walk. This was named for Major Shennan who used to walk his dog here. He helped Lady Buchan-Hepburn in the early days of creating the garden and the path is lined with meconopsis, primulas and rhododendrons. It is a favourite walkway for the peacocks that strut along the path trailing their spectacular blue and green tails. They also congregate around the duck pond, a serene flat pool with wonderful views of the hills above the River Tweed. Ospreys breed in the area and cameras relay pictures of the nesting site to a hut near the duck Pond. It is a reminder that the cultivated and the wild, the exotic and the native live happily side-by-side at Kailzie.

left (top): *An intimate little parterre of box diamonds and cones.*
left (centre): *Azaleas waft a heady scent along the woodland paths.*
left (bottom): *A wisteria casts shade in the greenhouse.*
opposite: *Drifts of* Primula pulverulenta *in front of huge gunnera leaves.*

above: *This old sundial was designed by A. Adie of Edinburgh in 1811.*
right: *A peacock struts his way down the Major's Walk.*
opposite: *Magnificent views of the Tweed valley are seen beyond the double herbaceous borders in July, with yellow loosestrife and Geranium psilostemun in the foreground.*

Lindisfarne Castle Garden

THE HOLY ISLAND OF LINDISFARNE becomes a true island twice a day when its two-mile long causeway is flooded by the tide. A feeling of closeness to the elements, coupled with a long spiritual history, gives it an ethereal quality that is strongest when the many visitors have left. The causeway stretches across the flat bay, its white-painted refuge box the only place for those who have misjudged the tide. Curlews utter their plaintive cry, cormorants dry their wings on wooden posts, and horses gallop on the wide sands.

It was on this remote island that Edward Hudson decided to convert the neglected Lindisfarne Castle on its craggy rock into a home for entertaining friends in the early twentieth century. Sir Edwin Lutyens was commissioned to transform the defensive fort into a comfortable house in the

above: *Abundant annuals with, to the right, white* Chrysanthemum coronarium.
opposite: *The sea can be glimpsed beyond the little walled garden.*

Arts and Crafts style, which he did using beautiful craftsmanship in a mixture of materials; herringbone bricks in the floor, stone slabs, simple carved wood and white walls. For a garden to complement the castle's interior design, Hudson turned to Gertrude Jekyll who regularly contributed to his magazine, *Country Life*. The creative partnership of Lutyens and Jekyll was already well known to readers of the magazine.

The crag on which the castle stands makes a natural rock garden, colourful in summer with wild thyme, viper's bugloss, stonecrop, thrift and red valerian. Gertrude Jekyll tried to further enhance this by planting flowers with the help of a lad from the village. He was lowered out of the castle windows and down the rock face in a pannier basket but it was not much of a success. The garden she did design,

however, lies to the north of the castle across a shallow dip in the thin, sheep-cropped turf. The summer colours of the plants shine out to be seen from the narrow, leaded windows of the castle rooms.

There was already a small walled garden, in which the garrison grew their vegetables and, within it, Lutyens designed a series of paths and beds that played with the perspective, making the garden appear larger than it really was. He also lowered the front wall to give good views of the castle from the garden bench. In 1911, Gertrude Jekyll made a planting plan, which still exists, and which the National Trust used when they restored the garden in 2002. Not all her scribbled notes were easy to read but as far as possible, the Trust have tracked down old cultivars to recreate her original vision as closely as possible.

The garden was designed to be at its height in summer when the family were in residence and almost half of it is made bright with vibrant annuals. Even on a dull day when the haar, a particularly raw sea-mist, rolls in from the sea, the large drifts of marigolds shine out of the gloom. There is a little entrance gate, weighted with a boulder to stop sheep getting in, and a welcoming herringbone fan of pebbles on the

ground. Looking in over the gate the impression is of a cool, grey channel up the middle of the garden, with flowers gaining in height and colour to the sides. This is down to the planting of almost three hundred *Stachys byzantina* or lamb's ears, their felted, silvery leaves giving the garden a cool interior.

Lutyens design for the paths uses uneven stones in varying shapes and sizes and there is now a slender sundial, very similar to the one that was there in the early 1900s, with the inscription, *A Timely Reminder Gertrude Jekyll 1845-1934*. Many of Gertrude Jekyll's favourite plants are here in the borders but, unusually for her, there are also wigwams and lines of sweet peas grown up hazel twigs. These form two screens to the east and west with a vegetable border behind one and a rose border behind the other. Pea sticks were chosen for being strong enough to stand up to the wind but pliable enough to bend with it. The only other height comes from wooden frames for growing clematis and a single tree of sea buckthorn.

opposite: Pebbles laid out in a Herringbone fan shape outside the gate.
above: *Double white opium poppies with blue cornflowers.*

Jekyll's planting is imaginative; double orange calendula marigolds contrast brightly with the silver lamb's ears, the same 'Orange King' marigolds look stunning next to rich blue delphiniums. There is a clever graduation of heights from the blue-flowered *Scabiosa caucasica*, feathery deep blue cornflowers, annual chrysanthemums, to the taller delphiniums. Many of the plants are delightfully unsophisticated: double white opium poppies, the gold-centred white daisies of *Chrysanthemum coronarium*, old-fashioned hollyhocks, and scented mignonette.

In one corner stands a garden shed with local pan tiled roof, a sweep of lettuces leading up to its door. The border next to it was described simply on Jekyll's plan as 'vegetables' and the Trust plant it annually with little rows of peas, beans, beetroot, cabbage, onion, artichokes and turnips. There are even tomatoes, sheltered from the sea winds by the east wall. Herbs include chives, hyssop, and sage, chosen for their mention in Jekyll's diaries. An irrigation system of drip pipes feeds the beds, making them easier to maintain in the shallow, sandy soil.

With so much of the garden dependent on hardy annuals, sufficient tough plants need to be raised before planting out at Lindisfarne. These are grown at Wallington and are hardened off when they are still very small, to create short, stocky plants with good root systems, plants that are able to stand up to the often fierce winds. This small garden is a gem, vibrating with colour in an otherwise empty landscape. It makes its own little island in the salty grassland, its skyline dominated by rock and castle, a classic, unforgettable view from the Northumberland coast.

above: *A copy of Jekyll's original plan is displayed next to the wooden shed.*
opposite: *The brilliant orange of cottage garden marigolds was much loved by Jekyll.*

Little Sparta

A QUARTER-MILE-LONG, gated track leads to the renowned garden created by artist Ian Hamilton Finlay, a mile from the small village of Dunsyre, tucked under the Pentland Hills. His house lies submerged in a green wood, looking inwards to its garden rather than out to the barren windy landscape. Over nearly fifty years, he made the garden into a work of art, rich with allusion and meaning and filled with some three hundred sculptures. Shortly before his death in 2006, he gave it into the care of the Little Sparta Trust that now manages it.

Thickly planted with native trees under which wildflowers flow into their cultivated relatives, Little Sparta is a contemplative space. It was named as a reference to the opposing cultures of Sparta and Athens, with Edinburgh being the 'Athens of North'. Many of the references are classical, with Latin inscriptions and figures from Greek mythology. Ian Hamilton Finlay's other main influences were the ideas and writings of French revolutionaries, in particular Saint Just and Rousseau. The garden and sculptures are imbued with meditations on the whole range of human experience: life, death, warfare, nature, home, love, food, as well as tenderness, affection, and humour.

The garden gate has high brick pillars, which carry a stone lintel, its face carved with the words 'A cottage. A field. A plough', and on the inside with 'There is happiness'. Ian Hamilton Finlay began changing the land around his cottage by digging out ponds, making waterways, planting trees and cultivating the earth. It is made out of the field, the plough a reference to 'the fluted land', an image that echoes the grooves on a classical column. Step through the gate into a green world where flower colours are subtle and soft; white from Solomon's seal and wild cherry, sweet cicely and hosta, light pink from hardy geranium and bistort, yellow from globeflower and wolfsbane.

above: *The words of St Just are carved into these eleven stones with the Pentland hills beyond.*
opposite: *The Garden Temple is reflected in the quiet pool.*

A square sunk below the level of the lawn is edged in astrantia with stones paving its floor, some inscribed with words. Around the edges of the lawn, little paths lead off into small groves, each with a different atmosphere, with different sculptural pieces. Brick is used heavily, as is stone, one man-made and the other from the land around. Sometimes bricks are laid right up to the trunks of trees, completely dominating the earth; sometimes the bricks form tenuous paths that are themselves dominated by grass and flowers. A quiet corner grove has dark stones and pink granite slabs on which rest hostas in terracotta pots interspersed with warships on plinths, a homage to the Villa d'Este in Italy with its much larger warship fountains. The tiny path leading out of it is a meditation on life and death. There is humour here too. A plaque below a small stand of sycamores reads 'Bring back the birch'.

From the sunken square, there is a green path to the house, lined with roses and currant bushes. Set into the grass are pink concrete diamonds each with the name of a type of vessel: ship, lugger, sloop, wherry, bargue. References to the sea, water, waves, and ships are often repeated in other parts of the garden. To either side are little spaces. A simple circular pool edged in *Geranium maccrorhizum*, dark green box balls, lines of raspberry canes with leaf-mould mulch, a touchingly domestic note, with camouflaged stakes painted in greens and pink. The theme is picked up near the house, where seven old salt-glazed farm troughs filled with strawberries are draped in blue fishing net with tall painted labels in pink and green reading 'strawberry camouflage'.

The cottage itself is overwhelmed by a wave of greenery, with climbing hydrangea, japonica, Virginia creeper, and wild elder lapping against its walls. Large wooden sailing boats fill the blue framed windows. An old barn stands at right angles to the cottage, forming a clearing in the wood with a large serene pool, fringed by many artworks; the pool and sculptures creating a whole composition. This is a calm, open space, the only sound a tiny tinkling as water fills a beautiful scallop shell etched with the words 'Caddis shell. Goddess shell'. Corinthian capitals edge the pool, its margins blurred by yellow flag irises, meadowsweet and kingcups. It feels entirely cut off from the surrounding uplands, a thoughtful, inward-looking space.

Against the old barn there are trained fruit trees, their feet washed in wild garlic, lily of the valley, and forget-me-nots. The Garden Temple at the end is dedicated to Apollo, its white-painted Corinthian columns reflected in the still water. Paths leading behind the pool plunge once more into the gloom of the wood. They curve sinuously between tree trunks, honesty, and woodrush. Variegated hostas in pots sit on elevated stones at intervals above the wildflowers. A sculpture of pan pipes reads 'When the wind blows venerate the sound'. Across a narrow, planked bridge over a

opposite (top): *A carved stone set parallel to the horizon.*

opposite (bottom): *A broken column lies in the rough grass.*

right (top): *The stems of trees become part of the sculpture.*

right (centre): *The words of Jean-Jacques Rousseau are on this plaque.*

right (bottom): *Claude Lorrain's signature on the terracotta-coloured bridge.*

119

stream, more brick paths twist this way and that, inviting constant choices and decisions.

Beyond the original boundary of the farmstead, a gate through a screen opens onto a network of woodland areas, streams, and pools connected by grassy paths. Ian Hamilton Finlay's imagery sprouts everywhere from plaques on trees, classical columns lying in rushes, carved stones and obelisks, running figures and even the stones beneath visitors' feet. Gardens used to be places where classical allusion and incised text would be positioned along walks, a tradition that he revived and developed. Alongside references to Greek mythology, such as the golden head of Apollo emerging from a meadow, are contemporary metaphors; hard-edged brick pillars have cut out shapes of battleships, a pair of hand grenades replace pineapples on twin gateposts, a pun on their World War II nickname.

Rhubarb was one of the first plants that Ian Hamilton Finlay set around the cottage at Little Sparta and here it is used plentifully along the streams. It fans its large, decorative leaves against a terracotta-coloured bridge inscribed with 'CLAUDI', which leads towards an upland loch and distant hills: a landscape reminiscent of Claude Lorrain whose 'signature' adorns the bridge. Above the bowl of the loch are eleven stones carved with the words of Saint Just 'The present order is the disorder of the future', lying in the moorland like scrabble tiles waiting to be rearranged. Saint Just, one of the principal thinkers of the French revolution, was sentenced to the guillotine by the very people he sought to liberate. The words seem to be speaking to the sky above the peaceful loch, the air filled with the songs of lark, peewit, and curlew.

Two rowing boats are drawn up on the banks of the loch where swans glide on the wind-ruffled surface, their feathers scattered amongst monkey flowers and yellow flags. A diminutive heather-thatched and sided building sits in a ring of paling fence like a playhouse. For some years, it housed geese, intended as guardians of Little Sparta in the same way as geese alerted Rome to invasion; but when they turned terrorist, they had to go. Round about lies heather moorland, tufted grasses and bilberry, a mown path tracing the lake's edge beneath three lonely Scot's pines. The way becomes moist and springy, a damp area of willows and alders, thick with scented meadowsweet, bright kingcups and furry flowered dwarf willows.

This is a more open area than that around the farmstead, with waterways flowing under simple wooden bridges. Here, the sculptures are open to the sky, not overshadowed by trees. A column lies on its side in the grass, inscribed with 'Arcadia, n.

top (left): *The golden head of Apollo reads 'Apollon Terroriste'.*
top (right): *Water gently bubbles in this lovely scallop shell sculpture.*
opposite (top): *'Never Enough' boat as sculpture.*
opposite (bottom): *The white-painted beehives stand with their backs to a small wood.*
overleaf (left): *An Ionic capital stands in a bed of wild irises.*
overleaf (right): *The thatched goose hut whose occupants had to be rehoused.*

'A *kingdom in Sparta's neighbourhood*', its stone cracked as some classical artefact, but its resting shape reminiscent of cannon. A dark grey metal wheelbarrow is dedicated to William Shenstone, eighteenth-century poet and gardener with whom Ian Hamilton Finlay had a great affinity. A clean white obelisk overlooks the hills in a young grove of trees, the names of wildflowers written on its base. These were the names of ships British Flower Class corvettes, later transferred to the US navy and renamed in typical US style as Fury or Restless, losing their romantic names.

As the land slopes back up towards the cottage wood, the grass has been cleverly mown to leave a raised ruff that traces the edges of an imaginary path. Three beehives stand with their backs against the shelter, painted as hives often are with numbers and names, their names proclaiming Bountiful, Sweet Promise, and Golden Gain. The names are of real fishing boats with their port numbers; they are an allusion to foraging bees and fishermen. It is a typically tender touch from a poet and artist whose work encompasses all of human life and aspiration and whose green garden in the Pentland Hills evokes a powerful sense of place.

Manderston

VISITING MANDERSTON is an extraordinary experience, a step back in time to an elegant, ordered age, and the gardens are a vital and integral part of this experience. The house was the setting for the Channel 4 series 'The Edwardian Country House', a recreation of life in a grand house in the early years of the twentieth century. For the programme, nineteen present-day volunteers went back in time to evoke the life of the new rich in the golden days before World War I. For three months, they became a family of five, looked after by a staff of fourteen in a house on which no expense was spared.

Remodelled in 1905 by the architect John Kinross, the house was designed to be imposing as well as luxurious for its owner Sir James Miller, a nouveau riche baronet of great wealth. The newly married Sir James wanted an impressive house that would also be elegantly comfortable, with gardens surrounding it which would reflect its taste and grandeur. To complement the neo-classical mansion, Kinross designed a series of four terraces of a suitable width and generosity. Manderston, now the home of Lord Palmer, is a unique entity of formal house and gardens, immaculately kept in true Edwardian style.

The front entrance faces north across a vast lawn, bordered by a sweep of pale gravel drive, up which it is easy to imagine carriages and horses arriving with a flourish. The lawn gives way to a wood through which a wide, mown path leads towards the Formal Garden. This is not a wild wood; like everything at Manderston, it has an order and regularity with its floor a serene sheet of bluebells in May. The gates to the Formal Garden, which Sir James had brought from a house in London, were gilded for him, so that they could catch the light from the setting sun. They form an impressive entrance to a magnificent garden that each year is laid out with thousands of summer bedding plants.

above: *Geometric beds contain floribunda roses.*
opposite: *The imposing gryphon gates.*

PLEASE
CLOSE
THE GATE

Subdivided into compartments by yew hedges, the garden has paths that lead between a series of 'rooms', each embellished with marble fountains, benches and sculptures. The vista from the entrance gates is of a long rose walk contained within box hedging and reached down short steps, guarded to either side by a marble sphinx. Off this is a square sunken garden with a marble fountain and a stone and wood pergola to one side. In summer red roses scramble up to the solid pillars in summer, through which can be glimpsed a second sunken square with a central bronze urn.

With quite a deep drop to this garden, there is room for rockery sides, which are smothered in the purple and yellow of aubrieta and arabis in spring. An adjacent garden room has echoes of a Spanish-style courtyard with its ornamental well and lead cistern containing daffodils early in the year. Nearby are the greenhouses and cold frames that are necessary for raising the vast quantity of bedding plants needed to fill the garden. At the back against the south-facing brick wall, fruit trees are carefully trained, the wide bed in front of them planted entirely with peonies, a glorious sight in June.

From the Formal Garden a picturesque cluster of buildings can be seen, amongst them the tower and the marble dairy which were created by Italian and French craftsmen. Beyond these buildings lies the Head Gardener's house, suitably grand, as befitted the status of this important member of staff, with its garden having a dolphin fountain and the ornate residence designed with a Scottish-style corner turret. The cool interior of the dairy has a vaulted, church-like ceiling and deep marble shelves for standing butter, cream and milk. The solid Tower next to it, designed like a Border Keep, gave good views over the surrounding countryside, and was a favourite place for Lady Miller to take tea.

As you walk back from the Formal Garden towards the house, the path skirts Manderston's very own circular cricket ground with its pavilion. A pair of fine, ornamental gates gives on to a short terrace to the east of the house, where there are four huge, garlanded stone vases atop tall plinths. Beyond these are a series of

left (top): *Raised benches give excellent views of play on the croquet lawn.*
left (bottom): *A fountain plays into a pool beyond red floribunda roses.*
opposite: *Terraces adorn the south side of Manderston.*

above: *Irises are planted in formal groups in the circular pools.*

right: *A pagoda amongst azaleas below the balustraded bridge.*

opposite: *The Swiss cottage.*

grand Italianate terraces, a magnificent setting for the south front of the house. There are two narrow top levels studded with repeated topiary shapes of cubes, boxes and half domes in yellows, pale greens and dark greens. Between these, there are flowering shrubs such as weigela, cotinus, and skimmia, whilst stone alcoves are neatly filled in with olearia or daisy bushes.

Steps drop down to the splendid main terrace, a formal parterre design made up of geometrically shaped beds containing vivid red floribunda roses and hostas. Topiary forms in yew and holly have developed some quirky, lopsided angles over time and give dynamic structure to the garden at any time of the year. There are two stone raised pools and even the four clumps of irises within them are formally planted with equal spacing. Goldfish swim languidly in the calm, flat water. In the near distance beyond the terrace, woods rise up vertically shutting off the landscape and creating a sense of privacy, of detachment from the world. Only a central gap gives a view of fields, copses and the far-off blue Cheviot Hills.

The edge of the terrace is bounded by a stone balustrade, the wall below it sun-warmed for growing ceanothus, wisteria, camellia, and magnolia. Tucked under a pair of central, descending steps is a shallow alcove with a bench under a long, low arch, a glorious place to soak up the warmth and watch swallows skimming the lake far below.

From the main terrace, the imposing Gryphon Gate leads to a croquet lawn, where shady benches on a raised bulwark gave an overview of the game. A pretty stone dovecot is set into the wall. The path dips down a long slope, past mounds of rhododendrons and grass thickly planted with daffodils in spring, towards the curving lake with its eighteenth-century layout. A bridge, with balustrade, covers the dam, the track over it leading to the far lakeside and the Woodland Garden with wonderful glades of rhododendrons and azaleas. A rustic Chinese bridge spans the lake and there are the sounds of oystercatchers, mallards, and coots amongst the reeds.

For his new wife, Sir James commissioned Kinross to design a boat-house, and the pretty, wooden Swiss chalet with its twisty chimney overlooks the lake. The informal, eighteenth-century landscape of lake and woods flows effortlessly into the stunning, Edwardian planting of the terraces around the house, making Manderston a unique place. There is so much to see, especially if visiting the house and dairy as well, that time passes very quickly. There is a sense of regret on leaving this extraordinary setting and rejoining the real world.

opposite: *Water lilies open their fat white blooms on the calm lake surface.*
right (top): *A statue of the Roman god Mercury.*
right (bottom): *Geometric beds contain floribunda roses.*
below: *A rustic Chinese bridge spans the lake.*

Mellerstain

ELLERSTAIN IS APPROACHED up a long drive of mature trees, where horses swish their tails in fields of buttercups and the limbs of an ancient sycamore are so bent with age they almost meet the ground. The eighteenth-century house was designed by William Adam and his son Robert and stands in a landscape created in the style of 'Capability' Brown. Visits to the garden are through a pretty courtyard of stepped gable buildings and clock tower with old-fashioned roses up its walls. A notice board describes what can be seen in the garden that day, such as 'azaleas and blossom, swans and cygnets at the lake'.

A narrow vennel or passageway leads to the south side of the house and the terraces. These follow Sir Reginald Blomfield's design of 1909 for the eleventh Earl of Haddington and are at their best in high summer when the roses are out. Immediately below the south front of the house are herbaceous borders of pink roses, lavender and silver lamb's ears, spiced up with rich red peonies. Roses and clematis are draped on the walls and ceanothus is covered in blue flowers. This top, lawned terrace has a long line of clipped, conical yew trees and a stone balustrade with double descending steps leading to Blomfield's parterre.

Under the steps is a 'crypto porticus', a cool space set back behind columns and looking out to the distant lake and the hazy, blue Cheviots. The parterre is divided into a series of beds sculpted from the lawn, with low box topiary in five-winged or in rounded, cheese shapes. There is a central path of beautiful rectangular stone slabs with identical planting to either side. Oval box-hedged beds are full of the scented 'Rose de Rescht', surrounded by borders of lavender-coloured *Nepeta* 'Six Hills Giant', a-hum with bumblebees and honey bees. The outer ring of beds is also full of roses: 'The Fairy', 'Bonica', 'Little White Pet,' and 'Cardinal Hume'.

above: *Sir Reginald Blomfield's grand terrace.*
opposite: *A fish swims languidly in the formal pool.*

East and West of the parterre are narrow mixed borders of meadowsweet, Japanese anemones, grey hostas, astilbes, and heavily scented white clematis scrambling over the walls. A pair of small flanking lawns create more-intimate spaces and a quiet place to sit. From the parterre terrace, curving steps descend to either side of a fish pool with balustrade and a lion's head fountain. Carp swim amongst clumps of iris, monkey flower and white water lilies, opening their huge mouths at the lichened stone rim of the pool, gliding like black submarines, silky dark amongst the waterweeds.

In front of the pool grow irises, their velvety petals deep brown and maroon, with golden marjoram and fruiting wild strawberries in the gaps between the paving slabs. To either side of the steps are purple elders, with roses and maidenhair spleenwort ferns against the retaining walls. Red-hot pokers are placed at either end of the grass terrace, carrying on the theme of symmetry. Shallow steps, smothered in ground-cover roses, lead to a vast, southward sloping lawn and the shimmering lake.

To the north of the house is a hidden garden, reached through a heavy pair of black iron gates and across lawns between parkland trees. The Thatched Cottage Garden is encircled by a metal fence and enclosed in trees and shrubs, a whimsical little building at its heart. With a white harled tower looking rather like a windmill and a thatched roof, it is certainly unusual for the Borders. This cottage orné, built in 1870 as a tea house, would then have been surrounded by bright bedding plants. A pair of stone frogs crouch by the entrance, and the path leads between two clipped yew trees.

left: The thatched cottage surrounded by box-edged flower borders.
below: *The formal pool beneath the house.*

A network of little beds is laid out with box hedges, their rounded profiles creating sinuous patterns. These are filled in with a cottage garden mixture of roses, lilies, perennials, and runner beans. It is a fantasy garden, full of charm and a complete contrast to the formality of Blomfield's parterre. Other features need seeking out, too; the dogs' graves, the fairy glen, the old boathouse and millennium pond, all tucked away in corners of the large estate. Mellerstain is indeed a garden of surprises.

right: *The lake sparkles in the sunshine below terraces of roses and catmint.*
below: *A cool white and green corner of the garden.*
overleaf (left): *Abutilons in pots at the foot of a statue.*
overleaf (right): *The unusual 'cheese' and 'fan' shapes in neatly clipped topiary.*

Mertoun

THE GARDENS AT MERTOUN lie mainly to one side of the early eighteenth-century mansion designed by Sir William Bruce and built in a soft pink-coloured stone. Positioned on a high bank above the winding River Tweed, the house commands wonderful views over the wide valley and is fringed with level lawns to the south, sheltering woodland to the north and east. The home of the Duke and Duchess of Sutherland, the gardens at Mertoun, while open to the public, are deliberately kept low-key. It is delightful to visit somewhere so lacking in commercialism and that feels very much a family estate.

Set in the formal lawns is a large pool, its edges softened with perennial planting, into which plays a tall fountain. Above its constant sound of splashing, there are the piping calls of the oystercatchers that often nest in the gravel path in front of the house. Beyond this, the steep bank drops to the Tweed, where one might see a lone fisherman standing up to his waist, casting into a deep pool. Meadows line the river, their margins tall with wildflowers in summer.

On the far side of the large pool are two sweeping herbaceous borders that curve into a central arbour draped with clematis, overhanging a blue seat with a cistus growing happily in the shelter and the light, well-worked soil. The borders look rich in late season, glowing with sedums, bronze fennel, asters, heucheras and edged in tumbling catmint and rock roses. A low wall protects their back, set with stone urns at either end. A tall Wellingtonia tree stands by the short cut between the stables and the house, to one side of the large pond. In spring, there is the heady scent of flowering currant bushes in which bees languidly work.

above: *Lupins and delphiniums against the warm pink walls of the old house.*
opposite: *The unique sixteenth-century dovecot.*

Behind the borders stretches the arboretum; established over the last forty years, this has a great variety of coniferous and broad-leaved trees. These are underplanted with massed daffodils that crowd around the cream-coloured peeling bark of birches and sweep in drifts far into the woods.

A low bank on the southern edge of the arboretum is particularly lovely in spring. Like a medieval flowery mead it is studded with oxlips in yellows and reds, little jewels growing in the short grasses of the turf bank. These were regularly planted by Alfred Breed, Head Gardener at Mertoun for fifty years, who distributed them year by year so that they now stretch along some fifty feet of the woodland edge. He also created the dense banks of primroses that crowd the side of the long, sweeping entrance drive, a nostalgic spring sight that is seeding anew thanks to modern strimming methods.

The path through the arboretum descends sharply to a little bridge across a burn before levelling out briefly then rising steeply again on the other side, where the walled garden occupies a south-facing slope. In the dip by the pretty woodland stream stands an unusual circular dovecote, shaped liked an old-fashioned bee skep. It dates from 1567 and is believed to be the oldest in the county. In its dark interior, which smells of age and damp stone, there are numerous niches for the birds to nest.

Nearby, on the outside of the garden, large climbers scramble over the brickwork; at their base is a huge spread of spring gentian, the most vibrant of blues in early May. There is a small wrought-iron gate in the tall wall, the modest, lower entrance to Mertoun's three-acre walled garden. Although such gardens were usually positioned some way from the main house and with a south-facing aspect, this walled garden is rather different. The land at the top slopes gently as is normal but then becomes a curving roller-coaster as it falls steeply downwards. At the centre stands part of the earlier mansion, Old Mertoun House, a pretty, pink-painted, crow-stepped building now occupied by the Head Gardener.

opposite (top): *Greenhouse and potting shed are back to back in the vegetable garden.*
opposite (bottom): *The fountain and large pool by Mertoun house.*
right (top): *The old house seen through lines of runner beans.*
right (bottom): *Geese graze on the steep slope in the lower part of the vegetable garden.*

The area that the irregularly shaped walls enclose is highly productive, reminiscent of a time when all large houses had working vegetable and fruit gardens. The steep slope at the lower end is verdant with lush grass and grazed by a gaggle of white geese, but as the land becomes less shelving there are row upon row of onions, carrots, potatoes, asparagus, rhubarb and every kind of vegetable for plentiful harvesting. Trained fruit trees span out against the walls, raspberry canes are mulched with straw, silver, jagged leaves of artichokes revel in the warmth, and fruit cages protect currant and gooseberry bushes from the birds.

A cluster of greenhouses and cold frames is used to raise young plants ready for lining out. In spring, they are full of trays of vegetable plants grown in plugs, as well as bedding plants and cut flower seedlings. There are many rows of daffodils and tulips, interspersed with the jazzy colours of polyanthus and the white caps of erythroniums nodding in the breeze. In summer, sweet peas are artfully trained up tall stakes to produce long stems for cutting, and these are followed by the warm colours of chrysanthemums in autumn.

There are abundant herbs for cooking too, the space allowing for a large, sweeping bed of the invasive horseradish. Room is even found for blackberries, which are neatly trained against the west wall. At the centre of this highly cultivated, immaculately weed-free area, the tone changes and it becomes more intimate as it nears the pink cottage that was part of the old house. Box hedge lines the narrow path and perennials grow informally under gnarled old apple trees. It has a charming feel, with peonies, monkshood, hardy geraniums, oriental poppies, and euphorbia.

It is the perfect place to live according to Head Gardener Jim Davidson, whose house lies surrounded by the colour of cut flowers and an abundance of vegetables. For the garden visitor it is a quiet glimpse into a private world, and an exemplary model of a productive estate garden.

left: *A water lily on the large pool.*
overleaf: *Lychnis and delphiniums in the summer heat.*

Monteviot

THE LOVELY TEVIOT VALLEY makes a superb setting for a house, and it was here, high above the river, that the first Marquis of Lothian chose to build his small, Georgian fishing lodge. From this original core, Monteviot has been much extended by successive generations, creating a fascinating blend of different styles. In the same way, the garden reflects the different gardening trends of over a hundred years and the present Lord Lothian, influenced by his world travels, is developing it further, and constantly embracing change.

Arriving at the garden gate, the visitor has little idea of the incredible view that awaits them. Before that, a cluster of greenhouses is enlivened in May by a long, narrow border of dwarf, pink rhododendrons, and azaleas, followed in late summer by sweet peas designed for table decorations. Beyond this, striped lawns stretch away to the homely house with its mixture of stone and pink harling. A yew hedge hides the view to the south but two fastigiated yew trees stand either side of an enticing opening. Stepping through here visitors are greeted by the unparalleled vista far below of the river Teviot making a wide, calm curve, a white ripple of weir in the distance.

The horseshoe-shaped viewpoint, and the massive stone terrace that it is set into, drop down sheer to a formal rose garden. This garden's rectangular box-edged beds are planted with hybrid tea and floribunda roses, aubrieta tumbles over the terrace wall and the air is headily scented in May by the cream-coloured, Warminster broom, *Cytisus praecox*. Shallow terraces above are planted with shrub roses and geraniums, with the pretty climber *Actinidia kolomikta* growing between the five-metre-high buttresses.

above: *Formal compartments make up the Rose Garden.*
opposite: *Primulas revel in the boggy conditions of the Oriental Garden.*
overleaf: *View into the River Garden with the Teviot beyond.*

From the viewpoint, the River Garden can be seen below as an irregular oval shape, curved at the top by a protective brick wall with sides made of yew hedge. Lawns sweep down to the river and the steps of a wide landing stage. Island beds are cut into the large expanse of sloping lawn, to a design of Percy Cane in 1960 and characteristic of the fashion of the time. These have recently been further developed to increase the range of planting so that there is now a lively mixture of trees, shrubs, perennials, grasses and bulbs.

Hard though it is to leave the viewpoint, a short walk along the top terrace leads to the south-facing front of the house with the original Georgian lodge nestling at its centre. In the shelter of the open-sided courtyard is a sunny herb garden with neat box hedging, enclosing rosemary, lemon balm, santolina, and lavender with a central sundial. *Clematis montana* scrambles over a low fence, smothering it with its open pink flowers in spring. Swallows dart over the courtyard, and roses and wisteria enjoy the warmth of the house walls.

To the east of the house is a large herbaceous border with a purple theme, protected by a shelterbelt of trees. The grassland that extends beyond this is managed as an informal lawn; at Monteviot there are six acres of formal lawns and twelve acres of informal lawns, contributing to an overall thirty acres of garden. Large drifts of daffodils grow in the rough grass, followed by plentiful ox-eye daisies on sloping banks under rowan trees.

The lower terrace walk passes through the enclosed rose garden and into the River Garden with its swirling island beds. These are planned for season-long interest with a backbone of gold- and purple-leaved shrubs and the silver of willow-leaved pears. A wide range of perennials is grown, with bulbs such as alliums and camassias; there are palms planted out in summer and foliage interest from hostas and grasses.

opposite (top): *The house forms a sunny open courtyard ideal for growing herbs.*
opposite (bottom): *A series of bridges links parts of the Oriental Garden.*
below: *Native ox-eye daisies make a charming display on this bank and are excellent for attracting insects.*

The curved brick wall was once used for growing peaches; at its centre is an unusual ornamental alcove with a green horseshoe-shaped bench. With its terracotta tiled floor and hint of Moorish arch, it is a wonderful sheltered place to sit and look at the river view.

To mark the millennium, Lord Lothian planted a laburnum tunnel connecting the River Garden with the woodland Oriental Garden. The laburnums cascade with gold in June, attracting numerous bumblebees to their scented flowers. The semi-wild woods can be glimpsed through the tunnel, bright with azaleas and bluebells, wild garlic and blue wood alkanet. The Oriental Garden has been made from an old curling pond, which used to freeze over in the cold winters, allowing the sport to be played on the ice. A series of four curving bridges link small islands, the gently rippling water reflecting tree leaves and water lilies.

The margins of the pools are gloriously full with pink bistort, hostas, purple *Ligularia* 'Desdemona', and brilliant blue meconopsis. These are interwoven with wildflowers, flag iris, forget-me-not, meadowsweet, and pendulous sedge. Vibrant pink primulas stand out against the greenery of lungwort, gunnera, and bamboos. Tadpoles mass in the network of small ponds and birds come down to drink. Tree ferns add a note of exotica, curiously juxtaposed amongst a sea of wild garlic.

Part of the woodland is laid out as an arboretum, begun in the nineteenth century, with additions still being made. There are cut-leaved beeches, walnuts, chestnuts, pines and Turkey oak, all underplanted with daffodils. In autumn, the arboretum is made colourful by the leaves and berries of many sorbus trees. The small burn that tumbles down through the trees is becoming a new Foliage Garden with two bridges built using recycled stones from clearing the surrounding potato fields. With block planting of moisture-loving foliage plants, it is a good demonstration of Monteviot's continuing development as a dynamic garden.

left (top): *The ornamental alcove in the high, south-facing garden wall.*
left (centre): *A hint of the Teviot beyond laburnums in full flower.*
left (bottom): *Cotton lavender and rosemary in the box-hedged herb garden.*
opposite: *Lush planting around the pool.*

Geraniums or Pelargoniums?

THROUGHOUT THIS BOOK there are references to geraniums in the flower borders.
These are hardy plants whose botanical name is *Geranium*, valuable in all sorts of
garden situations, versatile, free-flowering and supposed to be rabbit proof!
The tender, indoor plant known as geranium, which is also used as a
bedding plant, has the botanical name of *Pelargonium*.

Priorwood and Harmony

IN THE HEART OF THE attractive Border town of Melrose, there are two linked National Trust gardens, Priorwood and Harmony. Separated by just a short walk past the ruined Abbey, they are now being managed as companion gardens by Head Gardener Nick Brooks. Priorwood was originally part of the precinct of Melrose Abbey but has been run since 1976, when the Trust took it over, as a dried flower garden. With a band of keen volunteers harvesting and drying the plants, the extra income is used to maintain the garden.

Harmony, a few minutes away, is an older garden laid out around the 1807 townhouse built by Robert Waugh and named after his plantation in Jamaica. The house does indeed have a colonial feel with its steep flight of steps leading up to the front door, clematis draped over the railings and cascades of wisteria against the walls. The garden has tiny box hedges defining herbaceous borders and a front lawn that is awash in spring with nodding snake's head fritillaries. A stone-flagged path between cottage-style borders links the house with the vegetable garden and it is here that rows of flowers are grown to be dried in the sheds at nearby Priorwood.

With the glorious backdrop of Melrose Abbey, the vegetable garden is divided up in the traditional way into rectangles edged with box. Unlike an herbaceous border, flowers are grown in utilitarian rows echoing the vegetable plot. This is less surprising with the annuals such as cornflower, everlasting flower, and statice but it is unusual to see golden rod, hardy geraniums, and astrantia grown in this way. Many of these plants used to grow at Priorwood but, so the borders could be left untouched, they were divided and brought here to Harmony.

above: *The paved walk linking Harmony house and the vegetable garden.*
opposite: *Sprays of catmint soften the edge of the path which leads the eye up to Melrose Abbey.*

Many of the flowers grown for drying are unexpected. Plants such as peonies, euphorbia, bergamot, and chives can be harvested successfully and grow alongside giant thistles, yarrow, and sea hollies. Vegetables are still grown here too, but to make it a more visual experience the varieties are chosen for their colour and decorative leaves. There are rows of purple lettuces, vibrant chards, garlic, broad beans, and potatoes. Some varieties of runner beans have wonderful red and white flowers. Cages protect fruit such as raspberries, and even figs and apricots are grown outside against the brick walls.

On the unenclosed side of the vegetable plot is a traditional country garden border with lower growing sedums, catmints and lemon balm, rising to taller phlox, hot-orange lilies with stately globe thistles and tree peonies at the back. The stone-flagged path to the house has a pleasingly irregular shape, silver and purple leaved plants softening the edge and the cottage-style borders punctuated with tulips in spring and alliums in summer.

At Priorwood, the layout is satisfyingly simple, with one long rectangular flower border, wide gravel paths, and narrow borders around the outside. Amazingly, everything in this garden is capable of being dried, though now this is kept for display with the harvest being taken from the rows at Harmony. Lady's mantle froths over bricks that are laid on edge to make a zigzag pattern. Grasses are intermingled with the perennials, their soft plumes drying very successfully. Two large beds are sown with annuals such as pot marigold, poppies, and salvias and look their best in late summer.

opposite: *The flower beds early in the year with the orchard behind.*
right (top): *Sprigs of larkspur and astrantia with allium seedheads hanging in the drying shed.*
right (bottom): *A sculpture of three birds under the orchard trees.*

159

Beyond the flower area is a pretty orchard, smothered in apple blossom in May, glowing with apples in autumn. Some of the trees are quite an age and snowdrops, followed by spring bulbs grow in the meadow grasses. A long lavender hedge separates the orchard from the dried flower garden. From summer onwards, volunteers can be seen with armfuls of cut flowers ready for the drying sheds. They strip off the lower leaves, which gives off a delicious scent of new-mown hay, and twist elastic bands around small groups of stems. These are taken to the air-dry room and hung from wire coat hangers or along wooden poles.

Air-drying is the simplest technique, but at Priorwood, there is also a hot room where flower heads can be dried on wire frames or in sand. Large heavy blooms such as cardoons can be suspended through the holes in the wire frames. For sand drying, the heads are cut off the stems and carefully buried in trays of sand that has been mixed with a drying agent. All this produce is then displayed in aluminium buckets in the shop, or in the case of extra special and delicate blooms stored in racks of boxes. Even the beautiful snake's head fritillaries from Harmony have

been preserved; exquisite gems in muted, dusky purples, nestling in tissue paper.

The range of flowers that are dried here is staggering; steely blue sea hollies and rich red amaranthus, white acanthus and golden, flat-topped yarrow, lime-green lady's mantle and claret-coloured Joe Pye weed. There are many types of grasses to offset the colourful annuals, and there is information on the various desiccation techniques. It is an unusual way to plan flower borders, based entirely on the harvest they bring, and a fresh, new way of looking at the designing of a garden.

below: *A Scottish apple variety growing in Priorwood's orchard.*
opposite: *The marbled leaves of* Silybum marianum *behind a basket of flowers destined for the drying sheds.*

APPLE
GALLOWAY PIPPIN

DESSERT

Samye Ling

THE ROAD SEEMS TO CLIMB FOREVER up the long Scottish valley of Eskdalemuir, through a landscape of rounded hills that appear soft and green in summer, bleak and wild in winter. Passing isolated farmsteads, hamlets and woods, the last thing one expects to see is the golden roof of a temple. This is Samye Ling Buddhist Monastery and Tibetan Centre, the first and largest of its kind in the West. It was established in 1967, in the grounds of Johnstone House, a modest white-harled building whose window frames are now painted in the Buddhist colours of red, green, and black. The colourful temple was opened in 1988, and new buildings are constantly being added as the centre grows, under the guidance of its abbot, Lama Yeshe Rinpoche.

Samye Ling is a very welcoming place, open to all faiths and religions, and anyone can just pay a visit and wander in its gardens, whether or not wishing to participate in the life of the monastery. There are a hundred and fifty acres of land bordering the lovely river Esk and the gardens are surrounded by mixed woodland and meadows that even provide grazing for a family of yaks. On the lawn in front of Johnstone House stands a 'cloutie tree' festooned in fading strips of cloth. This old Celtic tradition is coincidentally also a custom in Tibet. Rags of material are hung on the trees with a wish or a prayer, which is taken off as the fabric fades. There are several cloutie wells and trees still in use in parts of Scotland but here it is a meeting of cultures from both east and west.

The flower borders by the house are a mixture of hardy perennials such as geranium, tansy and purple loosestrife, but there is little distinction between these and wildflowers or 'weeds' with golden buttercups loosely mixed in. The garden relies on volunteers or whoever is staying at the monastery and it has a semi-wild nature that fits its remote valley location. A pond is thickly fringed in variegated yellow flags and the tall bulrushes of greater reedmace, where moorhens call and dart amongst the greenery. Its central island is reached by a curving Japanese-style bridge, and below a tree is a small shrine, its stepped plinths covered in offerings such as feathers, coins, shells, pebbles, pictures, and ornaments.

Rising high above the pond is a massive white-painted stupa dedicated to world peace; white prayer flags emanate from its top and flutter in the breeze. From here, avenues of prayer flags are attached to tall black posts with gold finials and lead down a wide path to a circular lake set in a meadow of buttercups and daisies. Lily pads grace the lake's surface and ragged robin grows delicately amongst the reeds. At the heart of the lake is a statue of Nagarjuna, a second-century Indian saint on whose Buddhist philosophy is based the tradition to which Samye Ling belongs. Painted in gold, a large grey cobra spreads protectively over his head.

below: *Stormy light on the golden statue of Nagarjuna.*
opposite: *Parsley and basil, marigolds and lilies in the orange-painted Peach House.*

Everywhere, swallows skim the water or meadows, there is the evocative, bubbling cry of the curlew and sparrows twitter and cluster in the ivy around the house. Not all the wildlife is conducive to gardening but the problem of rabbits and peacocks is gently dealt with in the vegetable garden. Live traps made of wood mean that rabbits can be relocated and the resident peacocks are discouraged by low netting around the beds. Extending to about one acre, the organic vegetable garden provides food for the Centre and is managed on the deep bed system.

The season is shockingly short; the last frosts can be as late as mid June and begin again at the start of September. At over two hundred metres above sea level with reputedly the highest rainfall in the country, gardening here is a challenge. Everything grown outdoors has to be hardy except for the courgettes, given special treatment because of their popularity. There are rows of potatoes, turnips, swedes, beans, peas, beetroot, leeks, and Swiss chard with the golden turnips being the best crop of the year. Lines of yellow and orange calendulas are grown for their harvest of flowers and as companion plants to the vegetables. The concrete paths are edged in low mounds of the stones picked off the land and are smothered in stonecrop.

left (top): *Buddhist script amongst the grapevine in the greenhouse.*
left (centre): *Images of the Dalai Lama mix with gardening books and tools in the shed.*
left (bottom): *Prayer flags on Fairy Hill.*
opposite (top): *Tony's railway-sleeper shed amongst productive lines of vegetables.*
opposite (bottom): *A relaxed moment on the bridge to the Peace Garden.*

Shelter is provided by boulder stone walls on top of which grow hawthorn hedges that are almost submerged in summer by tall comfrey. Various enclosures are made; a sunburst of calendulas laid in a formal pattern, rectangular beds of herbs for harvesting, a netted cage for salad leaves, and a mandala of vegetable beds around a statue of Chenrezig under a copper pagoda. The fact that parsley can't be grown outside is an indicator of the conditions; it is lined out next to basil in the Peach House. Lilies in pots surround the base of a peach that was planted in 1997, the wall behind it painted a vibrant orange. Crowded with fruit, it does best if there is a sunny July.

In the Tomato House, French marigolds grow as companion planting to the tomatoes, alongside chillies, cucumbers trained up strings and dahlias for their fulsome blooms. Buddhist script is written over the door that leads into the second half of the greenhouse, a wonderful, snug place with lines of pots, old-fashioned scales and a faded chair. A vine is trained under the glass, and fig, nectarine, and peach do well here.

The vegetable garden, which expands and contracts according to how many volunteers there are each year, is paradoxically reminiscent of an inner-city allotment, in the wilds of Scotland. Recycled materials are used and this is particularly notable in the railway-sleeper shed constructed by Tony Freck. With its little potbellied stove, its tidy interior has tools, twine, shelves of gardening books, a collection of straw hats, wellies, gloves and, most essential, midge repellent.

The newest building is of green oak post and beam construction and will be used as a centre for Tibetan medicinal herbs. The College of Tibetan medicine based at Samye Ling takes a holistic approach to health and healing, and the burgeoning herb collection will be picked, dried, and packaged on-site. With its short season, this is gardening in extreme conditions, but it shows what can be done, whatever the site. The visitor takes away, as well as gardening inspiration, colourful

memories of this peaceful place; the winking of the butter lamps in their copper roofed pavilion, the reds and golds of the Tibetan temple, the cry of the peacock and the fluttering of the prayer flags; a little bit of Tibet in a Scottish valley.

above: *The cloutie tree festooned with fragments of cloth.*
opposite: *A small shrine sits on an island in the Peace Garden.*

left: *Nagarjuna's golden image reflected in the water.*
above: *Painted lettering in one of the garden walls.*

Seaton Delaval Hall

SEATON DELAVAL HALL once stood in many acres of farmland. Now on a rural island between urban sprawl and the sea, the magnificent mansion house looks out towards Blyth harbour with its line of huge wind turbines. Considered by many to be Sir John Vanbrugh's finest masterpiece, it is an outstanding example of eighteenth-century architecture, full of grandeur and atmosphere. A central block is flanked by two arcaded and pedimented wings that are flung wide like embracing arms that draw one in. Broad steps lead up to the imposing entrance, but inside it is quite a shock, for the central part of the house was completely gutted by fire in 1822. The stone and brick walls soar, floorless, up to the high roof and the sea winds now blow through the empty rooms.

The intensity of the fire can be seen in the thin, twisted remains of the iron banisters, but it is fascinating to see the underlying structure of a great house without the floors, plaster, or usual layers that conceal it.

Below stairs is a network of dark basement passages and storage rooms where shafts of light fall onto worn floors, some covered in carpets of hart's tongue and maidenhair spleenwort ferns. With the wind buffeting through the open doors, there are constant sounds echoing through the shell of the house.

The emptiness is exemplified by the view from the main entrance right through the house and out the other side to a hay meadow of many colours, red with sorrel, yellow with buttercups and enclosed in delicate iron railings. In the far distance stands a tall obelisk. As you descend the steps towards the meadow, the garden can be seen on the west side of the hall, sheltered on two sides by its high walls. Lord and Lady Hastings, the owners of Seaton Delaval Hall, live in the

above: *The parterre seen beyond a roof carpeted in stonecrop.* **opposite:** *Blowsy, sumptuous peonies contrast with the dark stone of the Hall.*

above: *The tiny Norman church seen beyond the crisp lines of the Rose Garden.*
below: *The large flowers of Clematis 'Nelly Moser' scramble up an arbour.*
opposite: *Stone urns and mounds of cotton lavender in the parterre.*

undamaged West Wing, and Lady Hastings has created a fittingly romantic garden for the house.

A large lawn curves around an old weeping ash, nearly three hundred years old, which, together with a box-hedged Rose Garden from between the wars, were all that were here already. Everything else has been added by the Hastings since 1950, including a large herbaceous border that sweeps around the lawn. There are hostas, geraniums, deep red astrantias, and blue meconopsis growing in front of headily scented azaleas and white-belled pieris. The glossy leaves of acanthus echo the Corinthian capitals in the empty hall. Voluptuous red peonies are mixed with pure white irises, the rather tender *Geranium palmatum* grows happily in the sheltered border, and pale pink foxtail lilies look stately in front of blue ceanothus. A carefully composed gap in the rhododendrons gives a glimpse of the tiny Norman church, whose simple, serene interior has a pair of zigzag ornamented arches.

The Rose Garden lies to the other side of the lawn, the highly scented roses enclosed in the fresh green of tall box hedges. From central circles the design emanates outwards in a complex maze of shapes, so while walking along, the visitor experiences different views. Each compartment holds a different colour of rose, with climbing roses and wisteria growing on the tall brick wall behind. At the base of the wall is a bed of pink, red, and white peonies mixed with white irises, a glorious sight when in full flower. It is even warm enough to grow bay trees outside in the shelter created by the house walls.

By a mossy statue, a small wrought-iron gate in a dark green yew hedge leads into an altogether more contemplative space. An enclosed and calm green rectangle of lawn is empty save for a square formal pool at its heart, surrounded by variegated hostas and white bearded irises. Goldfish swim languidly in the pool's depths and a little sculpture of a frog quietly spouts water. There is a pleasing formality to this simple garden with its blue summerhouse set into a curved yew hedge from which there is a view back towards the house.

Leading off the green garden, is a long laburnum tunnel, hidden from view until the

opposite: The statue of David slaying Goliath.
above (top): *Hart's tongue and maidenhair spleenwort ferns grow in the empty basement rooms - a 'garden' all of its own.*
above (bottom): *The blue-painted summerhouse glimpsed through a hedge.*

summerhouse is reached. At its end is a statue under a rose-covered arbour and all around are trees for autumn colour, planted to extend the season. Beneath the laburnums, there are alliums, their purple heads complementing the heavy yellow tresses of flowers above. Leaving behind the inward, meditative space of the green garden, a wide, sunken parterre, on the other side of the yew hedge, makes a complete contrast.

Designed in 1950, it was the first major commission for Jim Russell, who later went on to create the arboretum at Castle Howard. The box parterre runs either side of a long rectangle of lawn with a central fountain. Water spurts out of the mouths of three dolphins into a lotus-shaped bowl, delicate arcs of water also shooting upwards from a necklace of shells. A series of stone urns stand amidst circles of

grey-green santolina with other parterre shapes blocked in with lavender, purple berberis, red fuchsias and cascading white wisteria. At the ends of the parterre, there are exuberant scrolls and flourishes of box. A little green mount at the far end gives an overall view of these formal patterns with the hall rising up in the background. On top of the bank, a statue of Diana the Huntress stands next to a fine Ginkgo tree.

There is a feeling of theatrical expectancy in the garden of Seaton Delaval Hall that makes it so sympathetic a match to the dramatic empty house. What Lady Hastings has created is a garden of many moods, from expansive grandeur to intimate quietness, from country garden border to glamorous, heady Rose Garden. The result is a perfect balance between architecture and planting and an evocative garden that remains in the memory.

Teviot Water Gardens

THERE CAN BE FEW more challenging situations than gardening on a steep, sandy slope, but at Teviot Water Garden this difficult problem has been cleverly overcome. By creating a series of three terraces, the Wilson family have transformed a sharp hillside above the river Teviot into a mature, inspirational garden. It is not a large garden, but it demonstrates what can be created against the odds.

The Teviot winds its way through a gentle landscape of softly rounded farmland, past hedges and small copses before joining the River Tweed at Kelso. Here, the Wilsons have a garden centre as well as smokery where fish is cured over smoking embers in a large shed next to the old house of local pink flushed stone. Wanting a garden to demonstrate their landscaping business as well as the aquatic plants in which they specialised, the Wilsons began work in 1990 on the shelving sandbank below.

Many of the boulders came from local farms, and although a small digger was used, much of the stone had to be carried on to the hillside a bit at a time. It was a hard slog carving terraces into the unstable soil, building natural-looking retaining walls and sculpting a series of ponds linked by rills and waterfalls. Trees have helped to anchor and hold back the slope, whilst the beds are deeply manured each year to retain moisture and nourish the soil. The garden now has a permanence and fullness that disguises the underlying landscape.

right: *The garden clings to a steep hillside above the River Teviot.*

On leaving the commercialism of the garden centre behind, it becomes a different world, with a dark tunnel of box and larches heading straight down to the river. To the right, little paths lead on to terraces that twist around the bankside, paths that double back joined by steps, following the watercourses that cascade downwards. The first level has an irregular-shaped pond overlapped in spring by bright yellow kingcups. A waterfall that emerges from between lush hart's tongue ferns spills into the pool, which was made using timber stakes driven deep into the ground to hold the liner.

In summer, the pool is surrounded by the variegated grass Gardener's Garters, dwarf pink astilbes, and a large stand of bamboo. Acers spread their low branches almost to the ground, providing sumptuous colour in autumn. Early in the year, the beautiful double bloodroot emerges from the richly manured bed alongside dark leaved tulips and daffodils. The steep slope is held back by large mossy boulders where wildflowers are allowed to seed in the cracks.

The path descends, its steps edged in the spreading blue *Campanula poscharskyana*, polypody ferns and primroses. At foot level there is the top of a pergola carrying honeysuckle and roses, which, because of the incline, is above head height by the time the path winds down underneath it. There is a semi-natural feel to the planting, from clusters of self-seeding bluebells, snake's head fritillary, Welsh poppy, foxglove, and creeping Jenny combined with glorious blue meconopsis.

opposite: *Waterfalls and rills link the series of pools.*
above: *Huge gunnera leaves edge the pond.*

Further steps down are framed by large leaved variegated ivies and run parallel to more small waterfalls that issue into further pools. Here, a triangle of decking juts out over the dark water at whose edges bog plants luxuriate; reedmace, white skunk cabbage, dicentra and yellow flag. The colour of the water is echoed in an impressive specimen of the black bamboo, *Phyllostachys nigra punctata*, and brightened by vibrant yellow candelabra primulas. There is the sound of water everywhere in different tones, delicate tinkling, or throatier splashing from gentle rills and larger cascades.

Springtime in the Water Garden sees the slopes carpeted in lily of the valley and tulips in many different colours; white, carmine, deep red, purple. Bright splashes of colour come from *Primula inverewe* with its lively red flowers amongst the emerging leaves of hostas that enjoy the mulch of muck on the beds. There are plenty of other foliage textures provided by bergenias, ferns, glossy skunk cabbage, and the dark foliage of conifers. Looking down, there is a view of the lower level and a glimpse of the red-painted Japanese bridge, which spans two ponds in a low curve.

left (top): *Yellow Welsh poppies and azaleas shine by the water's edge.*
left (centre): *Primula and bugle - a combination of the wild and the cultivated.*
left (bottom): *The spring yellow of marsh marigold, Caltha palustris.*
opposite: *The red-painted bridge seen through the lush foliage of primulas, irises and hostas.*

On either side of the steps down to the red bridge are little natural-looking rills that tumble over saturated, mossy stones. A contorted willow drapes its twisting branches over the wooden bridge in suitably oriental fashion and there are views across both pools and to the Teviot beyond. Water lilies lie serenely on the surface and the margins hold white kingcups, *Primula rosea*, the white bells of *Leucojum aestivum* and the huge, spreading leaves of gunnera. A hedge of large-leaved bamboo separates the Water Garden from the wilder river beyond.

Fringed by reeds and wildflowers, there are river walks that follow the Teviot, mown grass paths amongst the longer meadow grasses. Daffodils line these in spring making an enticing walk past stands of silver birch, leading to a small circular turf-roofed building called the Stell. Early on, the riverbank is full of the white flowered *Allium triquetrum*, but when the grasses grow taller, comfrey, teasel, meadow cranesbill and Himalayan balsam take over. Swans fly overhead with noisy wing beats and mallards chaperone their ducklings amongst the tall reeds.

Walking back up through the Water Garden, though the path is steep, gives entirely new views of the many pools and borders as well as a chance to marvel at how this has been achieved in such difficult conditions. It is an inspiration for anyone wanting to garden on a steep slope, for it is the combination of clever construction and the quality of the planting that enhances it.

opposite: *The visitor building juts out over the garden giving an idea of how challenging the slope was.*
below: *A tiny waterfall trickles down amongst hart's tongue ferns.*

Wallington

ALTHOUGH OWNED BY THE National Trust since 1941, Wallington still feels very much a family home. There is a relaxed, comfortable atmosphere to the house, woods and grounds that ensures it is a favourite place in the hearts of many people. Successive generations of the Trevelyan family have remodelled the land, adding different views or features reflecting their own personalities. There is a lack of pretension to the house and estate, a feeling that it is a place that has been loved and enjoyed for centuries.

Essentially, Wallington has an eighteenth-century layout, with simple lawns and terracing on three sides of the honey-coloured house, a ha-ha offering views of the undulating fields that descend to the River Wansbeck. At the back of the house is the large, lawned courtyard formed by the wings of cottages and coach house joined by an arched entranceway with its pretty, little cupola. It is under this cupola with its blue-painted clock that visitors arrive, before emerging into the welcoming courtyard, where drifts of winter aconites stud the grass in February under a spreading sycamore tree.

A narrow border of roses and rosemary runs along the south face of the house, otherwise all is simplicity in order to lead the eye out to the landscape. The house is flanked to east and west by woodland, a broad walk leading to the West Wood with its three ponds and ice house. It was Sir Walter Caverley Blackett who, in the mid eighteenth century, laid out these semi-formal woods with avenues, paths, and ponds at the same time as restructuring the house into the building we see today. Curiously, though, he did not employ 'Capability' Brown who grew up in Kirkharle and went to school in nearby Cambo village, although Brown did have a hand in the Rothley lake area of the estate.

above: *The four stone griffin heads on Wallington lawn.*
opposite: *Allium seedheads, dahlias and Cotinus coggyria in front of the Owl House.*

To the east, Sir Walter created more woods as well as the China and Garden Ponds, modestly noting in his 1737 diary 'New gardens made'. To reach these, walk from the front of the house past a stone from the Giant's Causeway and along the side of a lawn on which sit four stone griffin heads. The griffins used to stand above one of London's medieval gates and they were brought by ship to Newcastle. Some of their broken wings pose somewhat incongruously by the China Pond, neighbours to Roman sculpture and a prehistoric stone. It is this eclectic mix, brought back from travels abroad by different generations of the family, which adds so much to Wallington.

The China Pond, so-called because Sir Walter, true to the fashions of the times, had put there what the then Duchess of Northumberland termed 'a very expensive Chinese building.' This has now gone and the pond looks very natural, the still water reflecting soft-coloured reeds or broken by the wake of moorhens. Standing at its edge is a remarkable tree, one of the first European larches to arrive in Britain from Austria. At over thirty metres, it was planted in 1738, a gift from the Duke of Atholl to Sir Walter who was planning the woods at the time. He also made a very large walled garden, which encompassed the long Garden Pond, but only the top wall now remains with its central south-facing gardener's cottage, known as Portico House.

To the east of this, Sir Walter made yet another walled garden and it is to this beautiful spot that the several paths and routes through the woods lead. The walls trace the contours of the land, enclosing a narrow valley, down the centre of which runs the small stream that has issued from the Garden Pond above it. Made of soft-coloured brick, the walls create a warm microclimate and enough shelter to grow less-hardy plants such as the Moroccan broom, *Cytisus battandieri*, with its pineapple-scented yellow flowers. Terraces on the sloping valley sides soak up the sun, and this, coupled with good drainage, means that phormiums, cistus and rosemary can flourish here.

Despite its timeless feel, the design of the walled garden dates back only as far as the 1960s. Replanted to a plan drawn up by the National Trust Gardens adviser of the time, Graham Stuart Thomas, it uses many of his favourite plants, roses, geraniums, and cottage garden

opposite: *Graham Stuart Thomas's beautiful colour scheme of blue and yellow-rich blue tradescantia is vivid in the foreground.*
right (top): *Fuchsias, ferns and pelargoniums crowd the staging in the conservatory.*
right (centre): *The urn and planters in the yew circle provide an ever-changing display.*
right (bottom): *Moorhen on the China pond.*

varieties in soft colours of yellow, mauve, and blue. Muted colours come from acanthus, *Crambe cordifolia*, campanulas, candytuft and aubrieta flowing over the retaining walls whilst on the top terrace are the hotter, autumn colours of *Crocosmia* 'Lucifer', purple-leaved smoke bush and *Dahlia* 'Bishop of Llandaff'.

At the top of the garden is a stone-rimmed pool, which is flanked by curving steps that lead down from the entrance gate. Designed by Mary, Lady Trevelyan in 1938, there is a small grotto at the back of the pond in which sits a sculpted horse's head backed by rough walls glinting with crystals. From here, the stream used to run through an underground culvert, known locally as a 'cundy', but in 1962 the Trust brought it to the surface so it could be planted with streamside plants.

Paths lead down the garden, sometimes crossing over the stream or leading into compartments hidden behind tall yew hedges. The little stream wends its way down, in places disappearing under culverts, before emerging into a larger, natural-looking pond surrounded by bog plants and set in the lawns of the wide, lowest part of the garden. Although a peaceful trickle on a summer's day, it was this stream that caused huge damage in November 1998. After many weeks of heavy rain, the outlet from the large Garden Pond above became blocked, the huge volume of water backing up before bringing down much of the west wall. The ensuing torrent scoured the garden as it raged down the valley. The National Trust had to source some 10,000 faded old bricks to reinstate the wall, which already appears softened with age.

The valley of the walled garden runs downhill from west to east and it is the south-facing terraces that can grow such a wonderful variety of plants, many of which need shelter. The top terrace is surmounted by a brick pavilion known as the Owl House after the stone sculpture on its apex. Adjoining this is the delightfully dreamy conservatory, laden with heavy scents and the sound of splashing water, which comes from a marble fountain set there in 1910, by Sir George Otto Trevelyan. It was he who also translated these lines from a Roman sarcophagus, which are carved into the marble and are so appropriate to Wallington's sunny garden: 'When wearied or over-wrought by study and affairs of business repair to these haunts and refresh your mind by a stroll amidst the flowers'.

top: *An invitation to 'stroll amidst the flowers' at Wallington.*

right: *The walled garden under a blanket of snow.*

The conservatory is a haven of colour and fragrance even on the dullest of days. Against the back wall, plants such as passion flower and purple bougainvillea flower happily. The staging is barely visible, cascading with tender plants, crowded with the multi-coloured foliage of coleus, exotic bulbs, and bright pelargoniums. Slender metal pillars support the glass roof and down these tumble the red and purple drooping flowers of long-lived fuchsias or the heady heliotrope filling the air with the scent of cherry pie.

Just as different generations of the Trevelyan family have made their mark on Wallington, the National Trust head gardeners have also added to the garden. Previously, Geoffrey Moon oversaw the 1960s replanting and excavated the large pond at the bottom of the garden. The present Head Gardener, John Ellis, came here eighteen years ago from Packwood House and recently, took an empty, square yew-walled enclosure and transformed it into a hidden Winter Garden. Bird feeders bring constant movement and activity to this sheltered space, viburnums and witch-hazels give off a spicy sweetness, the colourful bark and foliage of many shrubs is underplanted with cyclamen, iris, crocus, and daffodil.

Other 'rooms' in the garden are also created by dark green yew hedges; a large rectangle full of orchard trees and bulbs in long grass, a circle surrounding a central Italian urn, tumbling with colourful annuals in summer. Leading from here is Graham Stuart Thomas's masterpiece; a brick path sloping upwards under metal arches hung with the yellow flowers of honeysuckle, the path flanked by borders in a colour scheme of blue and yellow. A haze of smoky blue is provided by the catmint, Six Hills Giant, with spiky sea holly and tall veronica, and yellow shines out from evening primrose, golden rod and the trumpet flowers of daylilies. It is a simple scheme that is extremely effective thanks to the two dominant colours and the aged beauty of the old brick path; just one of the many contributions made over time to this lovely garden.

opposite: *Peonies in the mixed borders.*
top: *Mallard on the China pond*
left: *Red squirrels can be easily spotted from the woodland bird hide.*

William Turner Garden

PLANT KNOWLEDGE IN BRITAIN took a great leap forward when William Turner published his *New Herball* between 1551 and 1561. This important work was the first original book on plants to be written in English, hence Turner's accolade as 'the father of English botany'. His intention was to make it clear exactly which herbs should be used in treatments and would not put 'many a good man by ignorance in jeopardy of his life'. What made Turner remarkable was both his scientific approach to plants and his use of vernacular names, the latter making herbalism accessible to ordinary people. As he was born in the Northumberland town of Morpeth, the local council decided to create a garden to honour his name.

The William Turner Garden is tucked into a corner of the council's Carlisle Park. Away from the traffic-busy road, the park lies behind formal gates and is lively with spring or summer bedding. The shapes of flowerbeds are cut in the lawn, heady with the rich scent of wallflowers in May, with purple tulips standing in a sea of blue forget-me-nots. A large bank rises up the hill, thickly covered with mixed perennials and grasses and some splendid red-leaved acers. The entrance to the William Turner Garden is behind the greenhouses and a wooden aviary alive with chattering birds.

Walking into the William Turner Garden is like stepping into a medieval woodcut of an herb garden because of its strong use of wooden archways and simple rectangular beds. It was, indeed, from illustrations of the time that the design was drawn. The layout is spare and utilitarian as it would have been in the monastic garden narrow rectangular beds, each herb growing separately

above: *Spires of lavender and the twisted shapes of topiary.*
opposite: *The formaility of the Knot Garden looks attractive at all times of the year.*

On the sign in the photograph:

Chamomile - Anthemis nobilis

Turner used it to purgeth the jaundice
and healeth disease of the liver.
Used today in herbal teas and beers
and in shampoo for fair hair.

in its allotted place. There is a series of attractive information boards showing plans of the garden and information on Turner's life. This is a place of learning, but also a quiet corner amongst the busy life of the town.

There is a welcoming gazebo, square in shape, with damask roses trained up its stout supports. The posts are topped by tall, narrow pyramids made of wood, and topiary spirals are grown in large simple terracotta pots adding to the formality. Rosemary bushes bloom early in the year, followed by scented lavender. Wooden screens enclose the garden, all made of the same sturdy, pale-coloured timber, giving a strong sense of design. There are two levels, the first a Physic Garden, the higher one a Knot Garden with steps above that leading to a viewpoint.

William Turner was the first physician to observe, identify, and write about many native British species of plants, and the Physic Garden is labelled with each herb's common name and its botanical name, together with Turner's usage and that of today. The plants are grouped in sections such as culinary, cosmetics, heart and lungs, depression and dreams. Grown for their properties rather than their conspicuous flowers, there is an overall impression of green, especially early in the year, but this is soothing rather than dull. The names are evocative: good King Henry, Lady's mantle, bistort, mullein, and borage. Coltsfoot is included because it was used to treat lung problems and, here, the strict bed layout is useful to stop this vigorous plant from spreading.

opposite: *Sky blue flowers on the annual borage, Borago officinalis.*
above: *Each herb is labelled with botanical and common names.*

Many of the herbs, especially British natives, self-seed readily and the gardeners are constantly having to confine them to their original spot. Borage is a prolific seeder but its edible blue flowers are a delight in August. Chicory also has blue flowers, but these are large and ragged on tall stems. The cool green leaves of angelica curve over the arms of one of the beautiful benches, their wood a natural, soft, grey colour. Made by a local craftsman, they have unusual latticework backs made from thin, split panels of wood. There are other lovely details here; tiles that form a patterned edge to the beds have Turner's initials set into their pink surface or are decorated with an interlocking design.

To one side of the Physic Garden, a long narrow border contains some of the non-native herbs that Turner saw on his travels through Italy and Germany. Many of these look good in late summer, such as the steely blue globe thistle, pink wall germander, and aromatic wild sage. Planted at intervals in the bed are pear and crab apple trees, a wild pear having been planted by HRH the Duke of Edinburgh when he visited the garden in July 2001.

A short flight of steps leads to the Knot Garden. Simplicity is the keynote here, with little hedges of lavender, thyme, and box set off by a cover of pink granite chippings. Coloured gravels were often used in Elizabethan knots to emphasise their elaborate shapes. As the Turner garden is relatively new, having been created in 2001, there is still some experimenting to do with suitable hedging material. The frost-pocket conditions make it harder to clip tightly some Mediterranean herbs, and tiny yew hedges have now replaced the earlier hyssop. Gardens by their very nature are always evolving.

There are six knot beds, each with a central yew 'lollipop' and a few bulbs growing in the shapes created by the hedges. Lilies and white bluebells stand out against the pink gravel but, apart from these, the squares and triangles are uncomplicated by planting. The strict geometry of this design means that it still looks interesting even in winter.

left (top): *The superb lattice-work back to the bench made by Geoffrey Jackson of Langley in the Tyne Valley.*
left (centre): *Knot beds with 'lollipop' yews.*
left (bottom): *A medley of borage, marigold, marjoram, lavender and rue.*
opposite: *Lavender hedge in the Knot Garden.*

On two sides of the Knot Garden are wooden round-headed pergolas draped in roses and honeysuckle.

From here, the hillside rises abruptly with steep steps up the middle. On either side is a wild garden, where cultivated and native plants cover the banks. Primulas, periwinkle, and Solomon's seal are interwoven with cow parsley, herb bennet, foxglove, and dandelion, plants that have often formed a part of our herbal tradition. Seen from the viewing platform at the top, the layout of the whole garden is striking, in the same way that knot gardens were designed to be seen from the upstairs windows of the medieval house.

The town of Morpeth has its very own copy of Turner's Herball, which may occasionally be on display. It belonged to William Pickering, a Knight Marshall to Henry VIII and is decorated with lovely woodcuts. William Turner is believed to have gone to school in the nearby building by the bridge now known as the Chantry, so it is very fitting that this garden was laid out in celebration of his work.

top (left): *The wooden gazebo at the entrance to the garden.*
top (right): *Chamomile,* Anthemis nobilis, *with marjoram behind.*
left: *Detail of a sculpture in a quiet corner of the Physic Garden.*
opposite: *Tall, yellow elecampagne,* Inula helenium, *in the Physic Garden.*

Infrequent Openers

A NUMBER OF PRIVATE GARDENS in the area are open annually for charities such as the
British Red Cross or the National Gardens Scheme. Whilst only open for
perhaps a couple of tantalising days a year, three of these gardens are
so special that I feel they must be included in this book.
Blagdon with its fabulous Quarry Garden and the two great estate houses of Nunwick
and Lilburn are inspirational places with unique features too good to miss out.
Please remember though, that they are private homes, only open to the public on these days,
and check their dates of opening carefully with the charities concerned.

Knot Gardens and Parterres

KNOT GARDENS WERE especially popular in the sixteenth century and were made of
interwoven miniature hedges of herbs or box, best viewed from an upstairs window.
Larger in scale than knot gardens, parterres often have complex, intricate designs
made up of low hedges of box with yew, holly and box topiary.
Terracing enabled them to be appreciated from above and they were used
extensively in Victorian and Edwardian designs.

Blagdon Hall

A private garden open under the Red Cross Scheme and for Plant Fairs
or by appointment with the Blagdon Estate Office.

ALTHOUGH THE GARDEN at Blagdon is only open for charity on certain days of the year, it is well worth waiting for, especially for fans of Sir Edwin Lutyens's designs. A grandfather of the present Lord Ridley, he transformed several areas of the estate in his distinctive style and this, coupled with the lovely Quarry Garden, make Blagdon particularly fascinating.

The largely eighteenth-century mansion was designed by an unidentified architect and stands squarely at the hub of the wooded demesne with its long allées, vistas and lakes. A stream runs from east to west and full use has been made of its meandering loops, with paths,

bridges, dams, and ponds. The quarry, from which stone was taken to build the house, as well as houses and farm buildings for miles around, was made into a splendid garden in the same way as that at Belsay. There is even a full-sized cricket pitch with wooden, white-painted pavilion.

Lord Ridley's special interest is in trees and there are three National Collections at Blagdon; Acer, Alnus and British Endemic Sorbus. The scope is enormous; there are some three hundred types of acer, growing mainly in the wooded dene created by the stream, where their foliage glows in spring and autumn. The arboretum increases

above: The serene canal appears even longer due to Lutyens's clever design.

yearly and ranges from the tallest maple to that with the smallest known leaf, *Acer hyrcanum* reginae amaliae, which was discovered by the Tsar of Bulgaria and named after his wife, Queen Amalia.

Entrance to the Quarry Garden is through an iron gate below a pretty, white-painted iron bridge of 1789. To the right is a long lake adorned with two follies; a classical eighteenth century temple, and the ruins of a chapel with a stone coffin that were transported here from their original site a few miles away. The sheer quarry walls rise up above meadows of wildflowers mixed with cultivated plants. Hellebores, euphorbias, and perennial honesty enjoy the dappled shade beneath spreading magnolias and the leaning trunks of purple-leaved acers. Many tons of topsoil were originally imported by horse and cart to create the garden. Now the soil is naturally enriched by leaf mould from the many specimen trees.

The jungle effect of the Quarry Garden, which has its own sheltered microclimate, is further enhanced by festoons of *Clematis montana* which scrambles up into trees and rock faces. Here and there are sculptures; a Grecian style urn, its base hidden by grasses and wildflowers, an owl on a slender, carved stone column, a plaque on the rock, memorial to a favourite dog. Paths wind in and out, giving glimpses of colourful rhododendrons, their discarded trumpet flowers strewn across the grass.

Where the main path meets the stream, there is another iron gate under a massive stone bridge and the entrance to the wilder part of the dene. Here is the oldest 'tree' in the collection, a slice through a fossilised trunk, which was found in County Durham in 1998. It is set into the stones under the bridge and dated at three hundred and ten million years old. The margins of the stream are crowded with lysichiton or skunk cabbage, their fresh green fleshy leaves adding a touch of exotica. Red acers lean gently over the pond, whch widens out, its exit spanned by an unusual semicircular stone bridge.

opposite: *Slates laid on edge give a textured background to stone diamonds and circles.*
right (top): *Acer leaves in spring.*
right (bottom): *A cleverly positioned sculpted head seems to grow out of the quarry face.*

Vast drifts of wild garlic froth under the tall woodland trees and shuttlecock ferns open their delicate green vases.

Whilst the National Collection of Acers is mainly in the Quarry Garden, here in the more typically Northumbrian dene there are many varieties of Alnus, some sixty different species. Oaks soar above and swathes of Solomon's seal surround their trunks. There are other specimen trees, such as the Japanese Umbrella Pine with its very long dark green needles and the American hobblebush, so named because its rooted suckers could trip up the unwary. There are two further bridges, a high, black iron bridge built in 1881, and then a Japanese-inspired black and red wooden bridge slung low across the stream. The little valley then widens out to contain a pond and a small, secluded meadow.

From here, it is a short step to the old walled garden, which, in typical period style, was sited well away from the house. Blagdon's collection of sorbus is laid out in orchard fashion outside the walls, with daffodils in long grass around the trees and a mown path up the middle. There are over a hundred different taxa, of which twenty percent are British endemics. A circular pool, part surrounded by high, curving walls, lies to one outside corner of the walled garden. Designed by Lutyens, it is dominated by a series of dark Grecian urns on tall pedestals, a sombre and serious scene, which is lifted by the decorative paving. The gaps between circles and diamonds of stone are rhythmically filled in with slates laid on end.

The walk leads through an avenue of statuesque limes to a stone balustrade with two obelisks and steps leading up to a long path of millstones circled by bricks laid on edge. All this is also to Lutyens's design and typical of his attention to detail, many of the shapes are slightly different. An aisle to one side of the walk has numerous memorial trees, planted by members of the family or important visitors. One was planted by HRH the Prince of Wales on his visit in 1986.

above: *A copper beech leans over the graceful white bridge.*
opposite: *The ruined chapel brought stone by stone from its previous site.*

Stone steps lead up between blocks of clipped yew to the terrace on the south front of the house. The view from here is stunning in its simplicity; a canal, nearly two hundred metres long, again designed by Lutyens, who used perspective to suggest even greater distance by tapering its distant sides. The sky is mirrored in its calm surface and a sculpted pair of bulls, the family's symbol, guards the far end. The terrace has a generously wide bed of roses edged with lavender, where irises and purple-leaved *Viola labradorica* grow amongst the paving. The benches on the terrace are to Lutyens's own design, a very fitting place to sit and look out on the garden that he helped to create.

below: *Trees in the quarry garden give way to open glades.*
opposite: *The chequerboard path designed by Lutyens and a pair of narrow obelisks.*

Lilburn Tower

A private garden, open in support of charities at certain times of the year.

The house of Lilburn Tower stands on a gentle rise above a tributary of the River Till, with views of newly planted parkland trees and distant, undulating hills. John Dobson designed it for the Collingwood family in the first half of the nineteenth century as a comfortable country house with stables, observatory, and lodge. Now owned by Mr and Mrs Davidson, the superbly maintained and extensive gardens are a mixture of historical garden features and innovative modern design.

Intriguingly, the grand portico entrance to the house is arrived at through a vast sweep of wildflower meadow, a natural-looking pasture where the grasses are kept low by the semi-parasitic yellow hay rattle. The gardens are all to the south and east of the house and are entered through a heavy red-painted door in the brick boundary wall. This leads onto a long terrace, its striped lawns fringed with the deep purple lavender 'Hidcote' and white rambling roses tumbling over the stone retaining wall.

A pretty border of violas in lemon yellow, cream, and blue grow at the base of the conservatory, its glass whitewashed in summer for coolness. Inside, it is crowded from floor to ceiling in tender plants; begonias, bulbs, blue and white streptocarpus and pelargoniums sit in their terracotta pots on the Victorian staging. Fuchsias drip their purple

and red flowers from the delicate, metal pergola above and citrus trees hang with fruit. There are the enormous trumpet blooms of *Datura suaveolens* and a giant bird's-nest fern. The white painted wall is covered in purple bougainvillea and scented jasmine, with little tags fastened to the wires showing that biological control is used to combat pests.

Outside, the colour scheme of the planting is soft to allow the eye to drift to the far hills. A yellow and white border looks fresh and spring-like even in the heat of summer, with golden hop and white roses, white valerian and lilies, lady's mantle and the rhythmic, striped grass, *Hakonocloea macra* 'Aurea'. In the near distance, one can see a romantic folly, Hurlstone Tower. Named after a nearby medieval cross and built by the Davidsons in 2000, it won a prestigious building award for its craftsmanship. There is the heavenly scent of honeysuckle, which is grown to either side of the descending steps.

The land slopes to the east and drops down through a series of yew-hedged enclosures that were planted in 1932. Just below the house are the neat swirls and circles of a parterre laid out in the 1920s. Known as the Dutch Garden, its immaculately clipped lines of box are filled in with red begonias, and yellow, red, and pink roses. A 'hot' border

below: *The magnificent glasshouse was built in 1989.*
opposite: *The flowers on Thymus 'Pink Chintz' are a subtle shade of pink.*

grows at the base of the tall, brick, south-facing wall, a striking combination of orange Peruvian lilies, yellow foxgloves, golden day lilies, crimson astrantia, flame-red geum, and velvet-blue clematis grown on pea sticks. The wall is warm enough for *Solanum crispum* to flourish.

A double line of slender yew pyramids separates the Dutch Garden from the newer Well Garden. Designed by Head Gardener David Sinclair, this stunning modern garden sits very comfortably next to the 1920s parterre. The centrepiece is a carved, stone well with ornamental metalwork surrounded by irises in trefoil-shaped beds edged in stone sets. Circles contain pink standard roses, and beds of purple sage span the four corners. Everything in between is blocked in with carpets of thyme; a cross shape of white thyme, *Thymus serpyllum albus*, and the subtle, pale pink of *Thymus* 'Pink Chintz'. The effect is delightful and the thymes look wonderful in summer.

A twisting corridor in the yew hedge leads into a grassed area of lilac trees laid out like an orchard. Rising above it is the high brick wall that was once a double heated 'hot' wall, its chimneys still visible on top. An arched wrought-iron gate leads into the huge walled produce garden, which is still used for growing fruit and vegetables. Amazingly, even apricots are trained against the south-facing wall and in some years produce a good crop. In box-edged borders, black and red currants, gooseberries, and strawberries fruit under nets and there are lines of Florence fennel, courgettes, globe artichokes, beans, peas and salad leaves. Rhubarb is grown in the shade, and herbs such as borage and rosemary in the sun.

Fruit is also grown under glass in the magnificent greenhouse put up in 1989. It has two semicircular projecting bays, one a vinery, the other for peaches. The Muscat vines are trained in a sweep to meet at the roof, their grapes exhibited in autumn at the Royal Horticultural Society show in London. Pelargoniums are grown en masse on the raised staging and lemons hang

left (top): *The large catmint, Nepeta 'Six Hills Giant', creates a stunning vista to a white bench.*
left (centre): *The complex, maze-like shapes of box form the parterre known as the Dutch Garden.*
left (bottom): *Biological control is used to combat pests in the Victorian conservatory.*
opposite (top): *Detail of sculpture.*
opposite (bottom): *The house with lavender 'Hidcote' in the foreground.*

from trees grown in large pots. *Datura versicolor* grows right up to the roof, next to orange and yellow abutilons with their large, hanging, cup-like flowers.

A grassy walk under black metal Tudor arches supporting a luxurious range of heavily scented climbing roses, is another recent development. The eye is led to a white bench at one end and a pale marble statue at the other. The sides are fringed right the way along with the purple blue of the large catmint, *Nepeta* 'Six Hills Giant'. At the bottom of the walled garden and running parallel to this walk is the long sweep of an herbaceous border composed of muted colours. The white filigree of *Crambe cordifolia* rises above pink toadflax, blue penstemons, and silver artemisias alternating with pale veronicastrum and lime green euphorbias.

Leaving the garden behind, it is a ten-minute walk through the woods to a hidden Pond Garden. The drive, leading from the front of the house, passes the copper-domed conservatory and the bronze sculpture of a horse with its hooves blurred by grasses in the wildflower meadow. It then traces the course of the river, passing the ruins of the original fifteenth-century Tower house and twelfth-century chapel. The arc of a green-painted bridge, draped in wisteria, gives a hint of the garden beyond.

The Pond Garden is a delightful surprise. Edged with alders, its curving margins fringed with a mixture of native and cultivated plants. White foxgloves and male ferns grow next to exotic cardiocrinum lilies and the fleshy leaves of lysichiton, blue meconopsis are combined with variegated hostas, primulas, and shade-loving *Geranium nodosum*, Solomon's seal arches in delicate wands, and acers create dappled shade. The reflections of tall lime trees are mirrored in the still water, which is occasionally broken by a leaping brown trout. It is a world away from the formality of the walled gardens, but every bit as beautiful.

below: *Yellow hay-rattle is grown in the meadow to keep the grasses short enough for other wild-flowers.*

opposite: *The upper terrace gives a wonderful view of the immaculate parterre.*

Nunwick

This is a private garden open under the Red Cross Scheme.

SURROUNDED BY ITS ESTATE LANDS, Nunwick Hall lies in a small wooded dene created by a tributary of the North Tyne River. The pleasing eighteenth-century house faces south across ordered parkland, its lawns bordered by a ha-ha giving a continuous view to the distant blue escarpment topped by Hadrian's Wall. Centuries of tree planting have produced a special microclimate, which allows the stunning planting schemes to flourish in this often windswept part of Northumberland. Nunwick is the home of Veronica Allgood, who together with her late husband, Lancelot, has created some truly exceptional planting schemes in this delightful setting.

A love of plants is evident everywhere, beginning at the house, where generously sized diamond trellis regularly fills the gap between each of the two large sash windows. The house is clothed in ceanothus, honeysuckle, wisteria, climbing roses and clematis; even the rather tender Moroccan broom, *Cytisus battandieri*, flourishes here against the warm sandstone walls. The house is wrapped around in country house borders bursting with tree peonies, mulleins, and *Geranium palmatum* with its summer-long magenta flowers. A low retaining wall by the lawn echoes the hidden ha-ha and is aglow in June with cascading phlox, rock roses, pinks, corydalis, and pale pink cistus.

To the west of the house, a clock-tower wing protects an open courtyard, further sheltered by a small mount with silver birches and rhododendrons. An incredible collection of some thirty stone water troughs makes a dry home for tiny alpines that form neat hummocks over lumps of volcanic tufa rock. There are purple, hairy-stemmed pasque flowers, grey mounds of saxifrage, feathery erodiums, and tiny conifers making miniature landscapes in the lichened, age-worn troughs. Nearby, in the lawn, a fountain plays into a large stone basin, where goldfish swim lazily and birds like the spotted flycatcher come down to drink.

above: *A wonderful setting for hostas - the gothic folly of the Kennels.*

opposite: *Alliums enliven the massed hosta leaves in the walled garden.*

In typical eighteenth-century fashion, the walled garden is situated away from the house, tucked away in the species-rich woodland. On the way, a charming shelter, known as the Bark House, is a cool place to sit, its interior lined in split Scots pine bark, its roof supported in rustic timbers. Once in the walled garden, there is no shelter on a hot day, the neat rows of vegetables sloping gently to the south, catching all available sunlight. A deep stone-lined pool is the traditional place to plunge watering cans, and is sunk next to a fig house, which also grows peaches and nectarines with cymbidium orchids in raised wooden boxes. In further Victorian greenhouses are citrus trees in terracotta pots, shady vines, pelargoniums growing up to the roof and the deliciously scented cherry pie, *Heliotropium arborescens*.

As you look down the walled garden, the central path is edged with tightly packed rosettes of houseleeks and double borders of roses, summer bedding, and scented dianthus. A sundial marks the time and leads the eye down to a tall yew hedge, topped by five topiary cones, and a glimpse of the glass roof of the Camellia House. Once an orangery with underfloor heating, the sleepy Camellia House feels timeless. Bleached wooden chairs stand on stone flags surrounded by vines, wisteria, pelargonium and fuchsias, the soft jade paintwork has mellowed with the sun, and chaffinches fly in the open door.

The view of the burn is hidden by a stand of old yew trees, but slipping under a holly arch into the wood, one is suddenly confronted by Nunwick's most romantic feature, the Gothic folly known as the Kennels. Wrought-iron gates set in monastery-style arches lead into a series of small courtyards, each of the stone-flagged 'rooms' is filled with some of Veronica's extensive hosta collection. Their sumptuous pleated and quilted leaves, in every foliage colour imaginable, luxuriate in the moist burn-side folly. The walls are brought to life in June by the tiny fairy foxglove, *Erinus alpinus*, which seeds plentifully into every available crack.

Linking the Kennels with the walled garden is a beautifully constructed, two-arched bridge that was built as a memorial to Lancelot Allgood and is dedicated to him by a carved sandstone plaque. Two further bridges span the brown waters of the burn, one rustic and draped in Virginia creeper and actinidia, the other metal and wood and smothered in honeysuckle. The sides of the stream are lush with wildflower meadows, which have one cut annually in July to allow for self-seeding. Walking along the soft sawdust paths in June is a sensual experience, the air filled with the

left (top): *Miniature rock gardens are grown in a superb collection of stone troughs.*
left (centre): *There is enough shelter under the tree canopy for the Chilean Embothrium coccineum to flourish.*
left (bottom): *A black cat suns itself on the steps by Geranium palmatum.*
opposite (top): *Alliums, heucheras and geraniums ring the pretty fountain pool.*
opposite (bottom): *There is a timeless feel in the Camellia House with its softly coloured wood, and stone slabbed floor.*

scent of azaleas, the buzz of bumblebees, and the trickle of the burn. Buttercups and leopard's bane wave amongst the grasses on tall stems, white Queen Anne's lace makes filigree patterns against green ferns and young trout dart between the mossy boulders of the stream.

This garden is constantly developing, and a new bog garden area is filled with yet more opulent hostas. Lining a tiny rill, their rich leaves are mixed with bright primulas, jagged-leaved red rheums and the sinister spotted stems and curious flowers of arisaemas. The rill is fed from a stone sink below a tall pant that was rescued from sinking into boggy ground next to a field near Hexham. It is proof of the special microclimate of Nunwick that by it is a healthy specimen of the Chilean shrub *Embothrium coccineum* with its glowing orange-red tubular flowers.

The soft paths, using sawdust from the Nunwick estate sawmill, lead back to the outside of the walled garden and herbaceous borders sheltered between its bricks and a small orchard. Cottage garden plants are mixed with rare perennials in colours of white, purple, mauve and pink, teamed with silver, yellow, and the glossy red of peonies. There are the tight white buttons of Fair Maids of France, golden balls of globeflower, extravagant flowers of tree peonies and clear white of woody cranesbill. A pair of double borders is set at right angles to the path. Joyful trumpets of yellow, scented day lily reach out through deep blue aquilegias, Lime green euphorbias and plum red *Knautia macedonica* are bordered by a hedge of the Scots rose, *Rosa pimpinellifolia*. Nunwick is a real treat of a plantsman's garden, packed with interesting plants revelling in their protected climate.

below: *Silver-blue leaves of dianthus edge the path towards the Camellia House.*

opposite: *Miniature rock gardens are grown in a superb collection of stone troughs.*

Featured Gardens

These are the addresses of the gardens featured in this book:
Please use appropriate websites, Tourist Information Centres or local brochures to check opening times carefully before visiting the gardens.

Abbotsford, Melrose, Roxburghshire. TD6 9BQ Tel: 01896 752043 www.scottsabbotsford.co.uk

The Alnwick Garden, Denwick Lane, Alnwick, Northumberland. NE66 1YU Tel: 01665 511350 www.alnwickgarden.com

Belsay Hall, Belsay, Northumberland. NE20 0DX Tel: 01661 881636 www.english-heritage.org.uk/belsayhall

Bide-A-Wee Cottage, Stanton, Netherwhitton, Morpeth, Northumberland. NE65 8PR Tel: 01670 772262 www.bideawee.co.uk

Chesters Walled Garden, Chollerford, Hexham, Northumberland. NE46 4BQ Tel: 01434 681483 www.chesterswalledgarden.co.uk

Chillingham Castle, Chillingham, Alnwick, Northumberland. NE66 5NJ Tel: 01668 215359 www.chillingham-castle.com

Cragside, Rothbury, Morpeth, Northumberland. NE65 7PX Tel: 01669 620333/620150 www.nationaltrust.org.uk

Dawyck Botanic Garden, Stobo, Peebleshire. EH45 9JU Tel: 01721 760254 www.rbge.org.uk

Floors Castle, Kelso, Scottish Borders. TD5 7SF Tel: 01573 223333 www.floorscastle.com

Halls of Heddon, West Heddon Nurseries, Heddon-on-the-Wall, Northumberland. NE15 0JS Tel: 01661 852445 www.hallsofheddon.co.uk

Harmony, St. Mary's Road. Melrose. TD6 9LJ Tel: 01721 722502 www.nts.org.uk

Herterton House, Hartington, Cambo, Morpeth, Northumberland. NE61 4BN Tel: 01670 774278

Howick Hall, Alnwick, Northumberland. NE66 3LB Tel: 01665 577285 www.howickhallgardens.org

Kailzie, Peebles, Scottish Borders. EH45 9HT Tel: 01721 720007 www.kailziegardens.com

Lindisfarne Castle Garden, Holy Island, Berwick-upon-Tweed, Northumberland. TD15 2SH Tel: 01289 389244 www.nationaltrust.org.uk

Little Sparta, Dunsyre, Lanarkshire. info@littlesparta.org www.littlesparta.co.uk

Manderston, Duns, Berwickshire. TD11 3PP Tel: 01361 883450 www.manderston.co.uk

Mellerstain, Gordon, Berwickshire. TD3 6LG Tel: 01573 410225 www.mellerstain.com

Mertoun House Gardens, St. Boswells, Scottish Borders. Tel: 01835 823236 www.discovertheborders.co.uk

Monteviot House Gardens, Jedburgh. TD8 6UQ Tel: 01835 830380

Priorwood, Melrose. TD6 9PX Tel: 01896 822493 www.nts.org.uk

Samye Ling Monastery and Tibetan Centre, Eskdalemuir, Langholm, Dumfriesshire. DG13 0QL Tel: 013873 73232 www.samyeling.org

Seaton Delaval Hall, Seaton Sluice, Whitley Bay, Northumberland. NE26 4QR Tel: 0191 2371493 www.seatondelaval.org.uk

Teviot Water Gardens, Kirkbank House, Kelso. TD5 8LE Tel: 01835 850253 www.teviotwatergarden.co.uk

Wallington, Cambo, Morpeth, Northumberland. NE61 4AR Tel: 01670 773600 www.nationaltrust.org.uk

William Turner Garden, Carlisle Park, Morpeth, Northumberland. Tel: 01670 500777 www.castlemorpeth.gov.uk

Infrequent openers:

Blagdon Hall, Seaton Burn, Newcastle upon Tyne. NE13 6DE Tel: 01670 789621 www.blagdonestate.co.uk

Lilburn Tower, Alnwick, Northumberland. www.redcross.org.uk/opengardens & www.ngs.org.uk

Nunwick, Simonburn, Northumberland. NE48 3AF www.redcross.org.uk/opengardens

Acknowledgements

I WOULD LIKE TO THANK those people who have especially helped us in the making of this book:-
Billy Crozier, Jim Davidson, John Ellis, Terry Hewison, Lord Howick,
Robert Jamieson, David Knott, Gordon Low, Andrew Sawyer, Jessie Sheeler, David Sinclair,
Adam Stenhouse; and my husband, David, for his patience and long hours spent in
our garden while I was visiting gardens and writing.

Simon Fraser and I would also like to thank all the garden owners who have given their time
and allowed us to feature their beautiful gardens.

Finally, I'd like to mention my little tabby cat, Jack, who spent many hours
watching the computer screen from my lap.

Notes on Photography

THE MAJORITY OF THE IMAGES in this book were taken with 35mm digital SLR cameras:
the Nikon D200, and the Kodak pro slr/n. Nikkor lenses were used throughout,
with focal lengths ranging from 20mm to 300mm.
The images were recorded as Raw files, digitally processed in Adobe Photoshop CS2,
and saved as high resolution Tiff files. A few earlier images were taken with the medium format
Bronica GS1 camera on Fuji Velvia film, which was scanned on an Epson Perfection 4870 scanner.
A Gitzo Mountaineer carbon fibre tripod, with Manfrotto head and Linhof quick release plate was used.
A variety of light conditions were experienced, ranging from soft overcast light, ideal for
photographing plants, to strong sunshine which predominated during the hot summer of 2006.